COMMENTS (continued from back cover)...

Give-To-Get Leadership: The Secret of the Hidden Paycheck is both provocative and truly helpful for anyone who desires to improve their leadership skills.

At the mention of the word "leadership," too many executives take leave of their judgment and default to their own devices, leaving their employees, at best, continuing to perform at the level of the status quo, or at worst, frustrated and performing far below of what they are capable. Now, Dick Huseman and Merwyn Hayes have come along with a strong dose of common sense, mixed with wit, to bring things back on course. ***Give-To-Get Leadership: The Secret of the Hidden Paycheck*** is both provocative and truly helpful for anyone who desires to improve their leadership skills.

William F. "Woody" Faulk
Vice President
Chick-fil-A, Inc.

*More than a "must read" – [**Give-To-Get Leadership**] is a "must do" for anyone asked to "lead" others.*

In my position, I deal with literally hundreds of manager/leaders every year – from Chief Executives to Crew Chiefs – and if I could give them all only one book, it would be ***Give-To-Get Leadership***. Huseman and Hayes have produced a truly **useful** business leadership text. More than a "must read" – it's a "must do" for anyone asked to "lead" others. The **Hidden Paycheck**... can (and should be applied) in the broadest possible context – any endeavor in which we want to inspire others to give that extra "discretionary" effort. I'm sharing a copy with my Pastor, the current chair of our PTA and the leader of the crew who cuts my lawn.

Jim Collins, Ph.D.
Executive Director
Southeastern Electric Exchange, Inc.

Huseman and Hayes accurately highlight the hypocrisy found within most companies in how they relate to their employees – a hypocrisy that has killed trust… and choked off employee initiative.

Give-To-Get Leadership fills a hole in leadership literature by giving practical advice to real managers on how to improve their day-to-day effectiveness. Huseman and Hayes accurately highlight the hypocrisy found within most companies in how they relate to their employees – a hypocrisy that has killed trust and destroyed equity. ***Give-To-Get Leadership*** offers an alternative to the corporate elitism that has choked off employee initiative. Following the advice in this book, leaders can get on the road to securing a sustainable competitive advantage now and into the future – you've got to give to get.

Ken J. Perkowski
Former - Director of Executive Development
Mobil Corporation

Give-To-Get Leadership *is the key… to revitalize both personal and corporate success.*

In today's business environment, most enterprises are turning people off, not on, to the tremendous opportunities that are ahead. As a result, these enterprises are falling far short of their full potential. Drs. Huseman and Hayes have developed the blueprint for success in the new millennium. ***Give-To-Get Leadership*** is the key, and through its proper application and positioning, enterprises can again leverage people's ideas, insights, innovativeness, and discretionary effort to revitalize both personal and corporate success.

Robert Dorsey, Ph.D.
Executive Consultant
IBM Global Services

9/2004

To: Barbara

No matter what you do proffesionally or personally you will be successful!

God Bless,
Dianne

Give To Get LEADERSHIP

The Secret of THE HIDDEN PAYCHECK

by

Richard C. Huseman, Ph.D. and
Merwyn A. Hayes, Ph.D.

Cover design by Fred Terral (www.rightbrainterrain.com)

Library of Congress Cataloging-in-Publication Data

Huseman, Richard C.
Give-to-get leadership: The secret of the hidden paycheck
Richard C. Huseman, Merwyn A. Hayes
p. cm.

ISBN: 0-9712260-0-8
1. Leadership 2. Employee Motivation – United States
3. Fairness 4. Interpersonal relations 5. Coaching
I. Hayes, Merwyn A. II. Title.

Printed in the United States of America

Should you choose to be a leader, seek first to understand those you would lead and the field upon which they play.

– Richard C. Huseman, Ph.D.

ACKNOWLEDGEMENTS

Any book is based on the selective perceptions of its authors. All of us, in a sense, are prisoners of the ideas and concepts we have been exposed to. Early in our graduate school days, we were both exposed to the notion of Equity. In the decades since, that early exposure has been reflected in much of our consulting and writing. Like many of you, we have watched many "flavors of the month" come and go. But, despite our exposure to all of the latest "hot" practices, we continue to believe that the concept of Equity is the most practical explanation of human behavior – even though the roots of the concept date all the way back to Aristotle more than 2,000 years ago. It is this enduring quality of the Equity concept itself and its powerful ability to explain human performance which has caused us to anchor our approach to leadership (Give-To-Get Leadership) in what we now call the Equity Equation.

Over the years, we have had the good fortune to have our ideas tested and challenged by many of our colleagues in Fortune 50 companies as well as small start-ups, in both the public and private sectors. We are indebted for the advice, insight and suggestions provided by many of our clients. However, we alone bear the burden for any errors or distortions in what we present here.

We would like to give a special thanks to David Kohn for his weekly Friday "nudging" which helped spur us into completing the manuscript. This final draft has benefited from his editorial pen. Thank you, David.

Throughout the entire project, we have greatly benefited from the contributions of Zulema Seguel. Zu has truly been the project coordinator for the book. While continuing to do her other substantial duties, she has been the one to keep this project on track. Her management of the manuscript, suggestions, ideas and editorial support has contributed very substantially to the final product. Zu, we are in your debt.

TABLE OF CONTENTS

Part II:

PAYING THE HIDDEN PAYCHECK: YOUR ROLE AS THE IMMEDIATE MANAGER/LEADER

Introduction

Are you a manager or a leader? In the traditional, hierarchical organization, leadership took place primarily at top. Organizations were structured like a pyramid. Leadership was considered the domain of an elite few and your job, if you worked in the middle and lower levels of the organization, was to take orders, salute, and then carry them out. You served as a human exchange system for the information and decisions that constantly flowed up and down the organization. You truly were a "manager" of the everyday process.

No more. The old structure has been shattered by the poundings of the global marketplace. The pyramid has been squashed and a new, flat, streamlined organization has taken its place – one that demands much more effort from each of us. Today, for most of us, mere "management" is no longer an option. Regardless of your title – CEO, manager, supervisor, director, coordinator, etc. – if you have people reporting to you on a daily basis, then you have to function as a leader.

In today's corporations, decisions are being pushed down to the lowest possible levels so they'll be made and made quickly – by you. You no longer have the luxury of facing a problem and waiting for someone else at the top to solve it for you. This means you must be willing to make quick decisions, negotiate deals, structure work assignments, and grab at opportunities when they appear before you. To do this, you will very much need the help of the people who report directly to you. And if those people aren't loyal to you, then you're toast.

In the old days, people might not have liked their immediate manager. In fact, they might have even loathed him or her. But those employees could count on working 10, 15, 20+ years with the same company and in addition to getting a reasonable paycheck, they had the confidence of knowing that their jobs (and futures) were safe and secure.

That security encouraged many employees to put up with an inept or surly manager. The hassle of having to deal with sub-par leadership day-to-day in exchange for job security and a good pension for the retirement years was worth the tradeoff. So, employees remained loyal to the company, no matter what they thought of their immediate manager.

But corporate loyalty is hard to find these days. Why? Too often in recent years, employees have been left holding the short end of the stick in their relationship with their employers. They find themselves doing more and more work, and making more and more sacrifices, with little or no return for their efforts. Worse yet, many employees have seen their years of hard work and commitment count for nothing as they lost their jobs during an era of downsizing and merger.

In this kind of environment, people find it difficult to develop strong relationships with their companies. So, they are looking to someone else to build a loyal and trusting relationship with: someone they see often and work with day-to-day. They are looking to their immediate manager.

Yes, we mean you! You have now become the focal point for how people think and feel about their jobs and how well (or poorly) they decide to do them.

- The number one reason people say they *quit* their jobs is their immediate manager.

- The number one reason people say they *stay and like* their jobs is their immediate manager.

If you, as a manager/leader, don't have solid working relationships with the people who report to you, then you won't have their loyalty or full cooperation. You have to be able to depend on them and the effort they're willing to give you in order to help you make decisions and get the job done right. If you have only their heads and not their hearts – if you can't capture their willingness to give you everything they've got – then you aren't being an effective leader in today's work environment. And, one way or another, you'll have to pay a very hefty price for your lack of leadership.

Throughout this book, when we refer to managers, supervisors, etc., we are talking about leaders at every level of the organization, not just the people in the corner offices with big conference tables and panoramic views. In short, we're talking about YOU. We believe that it is critical that those of you who are responsible for how people perform at work on a day-to-day basis (be it one individual or a team of hundreds), realize that you have to be a leader, regardless of what your job title names you to be.

Our approach, which you'll see here, is very different from other leadership concepts. We refuse to focus on just "leaders" at the top and whatever competencies, traits, qualities, or other characteristics, these people may have. The people who focus on that type of *leader*ship basically have an attitude that in every organization, there exist only a few leaders and many followers behind them just waiting to be led. They focus on just these individuals – the select group that reigns from on high in the organization.

We think that this is an elitist attitude in today's business environment offering only very limited returns. Instead of focusing on just "leaders," we focus on developing **leader*ship*** – the collective ability to lead. Leadership, we think, is found throughout an organization, from the boardroom to the mailroom. The essence of leader*ship*, as we see it, is relation*ships*. That's why we concentrate on social awareness and the building of bonds throughout an organization. Leader*ship* development does not focus on what **the leader** needs to be effective. Instead, it concentrates on what **those people who are being led** require to succeed.

That's why we're targeting something radically different: **the relationship between you and the people who report to you**. This book zeroes in on how you can lead people by giving them what they really want from their work – and it's not just money. If you give them the non-financial benefits they crave, what you'll get in return is more performance and productivity than you have ever imagined.

So, what does this mean for you?

You as a leader...
...are the key to your company's success. It doesn't matter if you are the CEO or a front line supervisor. It doesn't matter if you work in a Fortune 50 organization or a small start-up company. You are the link to maximizing performance and profit.

You as a leader...
...are crucial to finding, hiring and keeping the best employees. Most people stay at their jobs out of loyalty to their immediate manager. That's you.

You as a leader...
...are the critical reason employees unleash their "discretionary effort," the extra effort and passion they willingly throw into their job when they're highly motivated and focused on their work. Almost any leader can get people to do enough to keep their paychecks. It's the outstanding leader who gets them to give their heart as well as their head to doing the job well.

You can get your people to offer up that discretionary effort again and again. In order to do it, though, you'll have to be ready to issue the **Hidden Paycheck** – those benefits of being in a job which aren't satisfied by what's in the pay envelope. Only you can pay the **Hidden Paycheck** to your people. Pay it out, and they'll give you terrific performance and profit. Hold it back, and your company may cash you out a lot sooner than you might think.

Don't consider this book a list of how-to instructions. Consider it a survival manual for the new corporate jungle. Follow it, and you'll find that the jungle can be made a much more gentle place than you thought. Ignore it, and you could be eaten alive.

Part I:

UNDERSTANDING THE HIDDEN PAYCHECK: THE EQUITY EQUATION

Every night, your most valuable assets walk out the door.

What guarantee do you have that they'll be back in the morning?

Chapter 1
Not Everyone Will Get It

Think hard about the people who work for you. Think about them very, very hard. Whether they're located at the next desk, the next cubicle, the next city, state or county – or even across the world – they are much more important to you than you may realize.

Think about this: Tonight, when they walk out the door of their office, or switch off their cell phones, what guarantee do you have that they'll be back tomorrow morning? More importantly, even if they do come to work, how do you know they'll be working up to their peak potential – utilizing the best of their skills and talents for you and your company?

You might have become a bit nervous while mulling over these issues. If you did, you have good reason. Corporate slash-and-burn strategies have crushed what used to be the cornerstone of the relationship between employee and company in the workplace – loyalty. In the past, companies essentially promised workers...

If you work hard and take care of the company,
the company will take care of you.

Taking care of employees meant the company made sure they'd have secure jobs, good pay, periodic raises, promotion opportunities, and a relatively worry-free retirement.

Now those concepts are considered meaningless, if not an outright joke. The era of downsizing, merger and merciless cost cutting has destroyed that loyalty – presumably forever. Employees have learned a hard and bitter lesson in terms of corporate priorities. That lesson, simply put, is...

Employees are not the company's first priority.

They may not even be the second or third. This fact of corporate life today has infected all organizations, even ones who have never adopted these loyalty-destroying strategies.

Employees in today's workforce have been put on the defensive. By being considered expendable, they have developed an unsurprising attitude of their own. It goes like this:

Treat me badly, and I'll get even.

This can mean quitting their jobs or worse yet going to a competitor and taking all of their knowledge, skill, creativity and talent with them.

An even more serious concern to companies should be those employees who have "quit" in every sense of the word except one – they still come in every day doing just enough to get their paychecks and go home. There are probably more of these people working with and for us than we would like to admit. These are the people who simply choose to do less or careless work. They seem to "check their brains at the door" when they come in each morning and just go through the motions. They take long lunch hours or burn up sick days. If you look hard, you might catch them working on personal business during company time and using company equipment. In very extreme cases, they might even sabotage the company or steal from it.

By far, the most common consequence for organizations as a result of the loss of employee loyalty is not easily quantified. It is very difficult to measure the number of opportunities lost to an organization because its employees are doing "just enough to get by." In today's ultra competitive business environment, no company can afford to have a team that is any less than the best or that does not have a passion for what they do. But, your challenge as a manager/leader is – even if you are hiring and paying for an all-star team – how do you keep your players from just showing up and warming the bench?

Here is the billion dollar question... after more than a decade of harsh corporate strategies that have more often than not left the employee holding the short end of the stick, is it possible to re-engage workers, igniting their passion and tapping into the best each of them has to offer? In short, is it possible to re-capture their hearts as well as their minds?

The answer is a resounding "YES!" How? By paying them their long overdue **Hidden Paycheck**.

We all know about the first paycheck and how it works: starting salaries, performance bonuses, annual raises, stock options, etc. – all of the tangible benefits we use to try and motivate people. There are plenty of "compensation experts" out there who aid companies in exactly how to negotiate and distribute the first paycheck. That's the easy part. Where organizations find little guidance is how to negotiate and distribute the **Hidden Paycheck** to their employees.

The **Hidden Paycheck** is not about money! It's about something that is frequently more important and always much less tangible in terms of what makes people tick. It's giving people, in addition to pay, what they really want from work, so they are inspired, not prodded, to do their jobs, better, faster, more effectively and more creatively. The currencies of the **Hidden Paycheck** include:

- Giving employees a sense that they're accomplishing something at work.
- Letting employees know the truth, that their work is meaningful and important to the organization.
- Providing employees a sense of recognition for their time, effort and dedication.

In this hyper competitive and cost-conscious business environment, paying your employees these currencies will do a lot for both you and the company.

The need for the **Hidden Paycheck** has always been there. People have always wanted more than just money from their work. But in the past, when companies gave employees a secure job, etc., the organization's loyalty toward them allowed them to feel they were part of something bigger than just their jobs. When they gave their minds and hearts to a company, it meant they received security and loyalty in return. Employees considered this a fair tradeoff and willingly participated in it. Now, though, the seemingly never-ending parade of downsizings, mergers and acquisitions has made corporate contributions to the **Hidden Paycheck** fall to near zero.

If companies would spend as much time thinking about paying the **Hidden Paycheck** to their employees as they do fretting over how to distribute salaries and stock options from the first kind of paycheck, they'd find that they would get a far better return on their investment – at virtually no extra cost. Using the **Hidden Paycheck** beefs up the bottom line far more than trying to improve revenues through slashing jobs and playing the corporate dating game.

An understanding and focus on the **Hidden Paycheck** can have a major impact whether your organization is in the Fortune 50 or a newly launched enterprise. Companies who want to stay competitive, to reap the most effort their employees have to offer, and to unleash creativity, energy and passion, will need to think long and hard about how to pay out the **Hidden Paycheck** to their employees.

BUT... There is a very important caveat to the **Hidden Paycheck**.

*The **Hidden Paycheck** must be issued and distributed by a particular individual – the immediate manager/leader.*

This form of compensation can't be doled out by an annual videotaped message from the CEO or a note from the Board of Directors. And it can't be issued on a quarterly, monthly, biweekly, or any kind of clockwork schedule. The **Hidden Paycheck** can only be delivered on a day-to-day basis by an employee's immediate manager/leader.

Surprised? You shouldn't be. Study after study shows that the key to employee job satisfaction comes from a single source: the relationship between the employee and their direct manager. That manager could be the CEO, regional director, mid-level manager or frontline supervisor. It doesn't matter. Time after time, employees say the biggest reason they quit their jobs is because of a "bad" manager. On the flip side, the most frequent reason employees give for staying with the company is the simple fact that, "I like my manager."

If you have people reporting to you, you must grasp one basic fact. Your employees don't form their opinions about the company by reading the annual report or surfing the company website. They develop many important perceptions and attitudes about the company from one source – you. Your employees believe what you tell them a whole lot sooner and a whole lot more than they believe the CEO.

If you are the CEO, then you need to realize that the people who believe you the most are the people who report directly to you. What those people in turn say to the people who report directly to them packs a lot more punch than you ever could. As humbling as this fact may be, if you're the CEO, your maintenance people will believe what the head of maintenance has to say about the company a lot more than they'll ever believe you. And so it goes up and down the corporate ladder.

Developing Leadership Versus Developing Leaders

While companies have changed dramatically in recent years in terms of how they structure themselves and how they do business, the approach of how to develop leadership hasn't received nearly as much attention. Our perspective on leadership development is quite different from most models today. The primary focus for traditional leadership models is to emphasize "the leader." They stress how one person can become a better boss by developing self-awareness, skills and competencies considered to be valuable in becoming a good leader. This point of view splits the world into two categories: a small group of leaders at the top and a large number of followers.

To us, this is a very narrow view of the role of leaders in the business world. Focusing on a select group of people for "leader" development can only offer limited returns. We see a distinction between *leader* development and *leadership* development. Leadership development, in our view, should focus much less on the "leader" and much more on the "ship" – as in relation*ship*. And, that leader*ship* should be cultivated at all levels of an organization, from the mailroom to boardroom.

This approach to the development of leader*ship* doesn't require military-like definitions of authority. Leader*ship* can happen with or without the formal roles of authority. Instead of focusing on a few people at the top and how they relate to everyone else, leader*ship* concentrates on interpersonal relationships and the building of strong bonds throughout an organization. This means that leader*ship* is not a skill for a few people at the top to learn – it becomes a way of conducting business throughout the organization where all members of the company are inspired to lead. The result: Everyone can be a leader, no matter what his or her official role in the corporate hierarchy.

Here's the crucial point to keep in mind. One person or a select group of people cannot possibly be the engine that drives an entire organization to productivity and profitability – no matter how much they wish they could. It's what happens during the daily interactions between the people at every level of the organization, which ultimately leads to performance – be it good or bad.

What is lacking today in most traditional views of leadership is an approach that actually connects "how to lead" with "what the people being led really need." Leaders don't operate in a vacuum. Before they can do anything, they need to think about the people they are leading and what will motivate them to do what needs to be done. Therefore, our version of leader*ship* development doesn't focus on what the traits "leaders" need to be effective. Instead, we target what those who are being led require – what they need to succeed all day, every day.

The Hidden Paycheck Challenge

So, here's your challenge:

- Do you acknowledge that this era of downsizing, merger and drastic cost-cutting has reshaped the way employees look at their respective organizations, with the result being that most employees aren't as loyal to their organizations as they once were – and that this loss of commitment and loyalty directly impacts an organization's performance and profitability?

- Do you recognize that, while pay, benefits and other tangible incentives will continue to play a major role in what organizations give their employees, "compensation" also comes in other important currencies (i.e., **The Hidden Paycheck**) that people desire and expect as a part of their incentive to perform well at their jobs?

- Finally, can you accept that the immediate manager/leader at every level of the organization has the most powerful influence on the performance and innovation of their employees – and that it is through these same immediate managers/leaders that the **Hidden Paycheck** must be delivered?

If you can say "Yes!" to all of those questions, then you have made the equivalent of a moon landing. In other words...

N	*O*	*T*	*E*
V	*E*	*R*	*Y*
O	*N*	*E*	*W*
I	*L*	*L*	*G*
E	*T*	*I*	*T*

(If you have trouble decoding the message, turn to the end of the chapter for the answer)

Remember, success in business comes from making the right moves at the right time. Suppose in the early 1980s, a booming voice from the sky had thundered, "The strategy for the future is to put most of your money into technology and dump half your work force!" You probably would have laughed at the idea. Yet, those companies who made those moves the fastest and the earliest were the ones who profited the most.

Now, however, the benefits from these moves have been pretty well tapped out, and we all have to live with their consequences. It's time for a new strategy – and it's not one that you can just pull "off the shelf" or some "flavor of the month."

Don't make the same mistake many leaders do who look for better ways of doing business by subscribing to the principles of "benchmarking." They believe that they can improve their organization's performance by first going out and "benchmarking" what their competitors are doing and then use that as a guide as to what they should do. What an interesting assumption! By imitating your competitors, you'll somehow end up with better results. You can use their plays and beat them at their own game. In our opinion, this can't and won't work. Benchmarking might keep you in the game for a while, but it can't give you the edge that you need to win.

Taking A "Contrarian" Approach

Real business breakthroughs happen when organizations decide to do a few things in a dramatically different way from their competition. Indeed, that competitive advantage is often achieved by doing some things exactly the opposite of the way everyone else is doing them. It's a bit like playing the stock market. Sometimes you can make the most money by buying when everyone else is selling, and selling when everyone else is buying.

So, if you, as a manager/leader, want to have a real impact and you want high-voltage results, then it's time to think out of the box. You need to focus less on doing things *better* and a lot more on doing a few things *differently*. Now is the time for a striking new approach. It's time to dump those command-and-control attitudes, where managers and leaders act like a driver whipping a team of horses hard and fast to keep them in enough fear and pain to win the race.

Really think about what you and your organization might gain if, while everyone else is dumping employees like used-up parts whenever the bottom line needs a short-term boost (Think that's an exaggeration? In 2000, downsizing hit 1.84 million people), you decide to do something radically different.

Suppose you decide to put a premium on keeping and growing employees – whether it's at the corporate level or just within your own team? What if you decide you're going to have a laser-like focus on inspiring the maximum amount of performance and the highest form of innovation you can get from your employees by zeroing in on having long-term and productive relationships with them? How about if you actually invest in the foundation of your success – the people who do the work and make things happen every day?

The only way you can adapt, survive and excel in today's turbulent business environment is by virtue of the effort the people who work for you put into the organization.

Your job is to get the best effort and creativity you're your employees can give. This book will help you do it.

How?

By getting you ready to maximize a new performance standard for this new millennium – the **Hidden Paycheck**. The **Hidden Paycheck** pays off for everyone. It gives your employees what they really want from their work and gives you what you want – high performance and plump profits you can point to with pride.

The message on page 13 becomes clear when you read the first word as "not." The message then quickly reads, "Not everyone will get it." There is always a competitive advantage to gaining insight before your competition. Imagine the advantage you'll gain if "you get it" before they do.

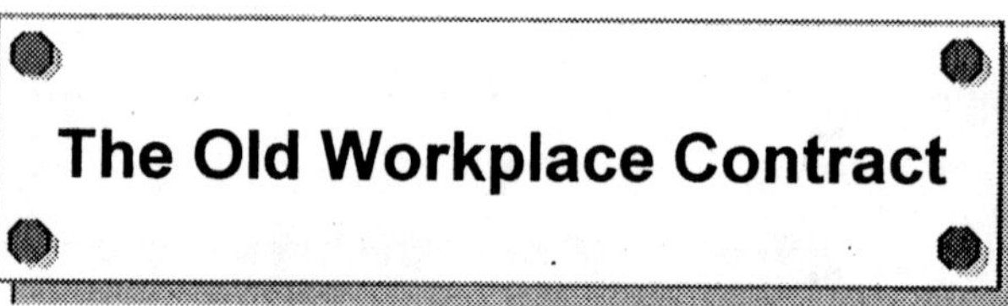

If you work hard and
take care of the company,
the company will take care of you.

Chapter 2
The Demise of the Old Workplace Contract

Once upon a time, in a land not so far away, we all lived in world that was stable, constant and certain. We knew that, just as sure as there were death and taxes, if we worked hard and did our jobs the best we knew how, that raises, promotions and a golden retirement would be showered upon us.

American corporations were on top of the world. Our business leaders were the top players across the entire globe no matter what industry they represented. Our companies invented new products almost as quickly as raindrops fall, and the profits our companies accumulated would have made Solomon blush. American companies were not only on top of the world – they ran it. That success meant our jobs were safe, secure, and our paychecks were guaranteed. We were living the American Dream and we reveled in it.

While we were dreaming, though, reality began to nibble at the edges of our lives. Suddenly, business leaders from other countries started to become major players. Foreign companies not only made better gizmos than we did, they made things we hadn't even thought of yet and they did it faster. Suddenly our dreams were turning into a nightmare, one that threatened the survival of our economy, our companies, and our jobs.

The facts were clear:

- In 1960, 70 of the top 100 industrial companies in the world were based in the U.S.

- By 1995, the number of American companies in the top 100 had slid to only 24.

The dream of American corporate dominance had kept many leaders slumbering in their complacency. The real world, however, had become a very different place. Suddenly, success was based on being nimble in the global marketplace. Business leaders found they had to keep themselves on top of the changes in exponentially changing technology and markets. Even worse, they had to manage and deploy this new technology in those markets. The companies just awakening from their slumber had to do something – and do it fast.

Reengineering: A Strategy For Survival

Suddenly, the buzzword on everyone's lips was corporate "reengineering." The reengineering movement wrapped itself around change and held the key to survival. There were three major elements to it. Change had to be fundamental, radical and dramatic.

Fundamental: Organizations could take nothing for granted. They had to question even the most basic aspects of how they did business.

Radical: Organizations had to rethink everything and do radical surgery on the ways in which they operated, both inside and outside the company.

Dramatic: Incremental change, which just tinkered with existing procedures and ideas, was no longer acceptable. Now, quantum leaps in performance were the order of the day.

With these reengineering principles in the forefront of their thoughts, leaders within each company began to look for specific strategies that would allow them to run past the competition -- and once out in front, that would let them maintain their lead.

Two major strategies emerged. Companies could either ***shrink*** or ***transact*** their way back to the top.

Shrinking for Success

By the end of World War II, many American companies were run like the military. Every worker had a specific assignment and there was layer upon layer of hierarchy. For every task, there was someone assigned to it. For every group of people performing tasks, there was a manager looking over their shoulders to make sure the job got done. A highly structured system for overseeing employees was the way to make sure the company operated at peak efficiency.

Then, as the global marketplace changed, the companies who had been thought of as mighty colossuses, suddenly looked like lumbering, wheezing giants. Their profits slid, and so did their position in their industry. Suddenly, rapid technological changes and highly volatile markets became everyday fare, and companies had to be lean and mean in order to keep up. The number of employees had to be reduced and cherished bureaucracies had to be battered and broken.

But there was a price to be paid. CEOs and their leadership teams were acutely aware of the loyalty they had engendered in their workers – the confidence that if an employee worked hard and took care of the company, the company had a responsibility to take care of them. But leaders became convinced they had to shed workers, no matter what the price.

Many leaders winced as they first ordered thousands of people be given pink slips. In the beginning, those who were let go often received decent severance packages. Benefits were continued and pensions were honored. Even so, the public began a huge and pained outcry at this massive wielding of the corporate axe. They couldn't believe that companies were backing out of the "employment for life" contracts they had promised their workers.

To be fair, layoffs were not new. They had been used in the past. However, they had been tied to the overall economy and to industry business cycles. If a company laid off employees, it was only because the economy was sagging and people weren't buying as many refrigerators as before. It made sense that during these down cycles, companies would be forced to let some of their people go temporarily. When times improved, many of those same workers were rehired. The public understood this as one of the realities of corporate life.

A prime case in point was the auto industry. When times were flush and people were buying cars every couple of years, the production lines were humming and the car companies hired more workers. When times slowed and showrooms stood empty, the companies laid off workers because fewer people were buying cars.

However, during the decade of the 1990's, business cycles were no longer the major reason companies engaged in downsizing. American Management Association polls showed that the change was sudden and dramatic.

- In 1990-1991, 73% of companies engaged in layoffs because of business downturns.

- By 1992-1993, that number was 66%.

- In 1995-1996, only 36.6% of companies said they were laying off people because of business downturns.

So, while the actual number of layoffs continued to climb dramatically, companies apparently had another reason for dumping their people. What was this reason? Companies needed to quickly boost profits and the price of their stock.

Some companies tried to cloak their real reasons for letting people go under such benign sounding terms as "rightsizing" or "reengineering." No matter what they called it, however, companies using these approaches were attacked, especially by the media, for betraying the employees who had depended on them for a secure job and the promise of a generous pension.

However, in 1993, something happened that opened the door for downsizing to become a much more broadly accepted business strategy. For years, IBM was considered THE corporate role model – they represented the ideal when it came to how a classical and extremely successful corporation should function and operate.

For decades, IBM had resembled a state-run company with lifetime employment and a strong social contract between management and labor. IBM gave its workers excellent health insurance, education and pension benefits. They also offered their people company golf courses, childcare and even mortgage assistance. More importantly, IBM provided a lifetime ladder of employment with every career step carefully laid out and secured. IBM employees worked under the utmost corporate loyalty protection:

If you work hard for Big Blue and take care of the company, Big Blue will take care of you.

Then, however, the unthinkable happened. Whereas IBM had racked up the largest American corporate profit only eight years before, in 1992, the company suffered a massive loss of over $6.6 billion. As a result, in July of 1993, Big Blue announced that it would "trim" its workforce by 31,000 employees.

The aftershocks struck every boardroom in America. By breaking their corporate loyalty promise to their employees, IBM opened the door for other companies to do the same. "If IBM can do it, so can we," became the corporate battle cry. With renewed confidence, companies began shedding tens of thousands of jobs, pushing people out into the street – people who thought they had their jobs until retirement.

So, what was the impact on all of the people who suddenly found themselves scrambling to survive? They ended up paying a very hefty price for their corporate loyalty.

For those people lucky enough to find new jobs, they first had to bear the cost of retraining themselves to even make themselves "employable" to other companies. Many had to work two or more jobs and still were not making as much as they did before they were let go. Financial stress caused marriages to fall apart. Parents had to tell their kids that they couldn't afford to send them

Two Views of Big Blue News

From the Glenn Falls Post-Star
March 11, 1994

IBM Corp., as part of its goal to cut over 30,000 jobs in this year, laid off 800 New York workers Thursday. . .

IBM announced that it would trim its work force from 256,000 to 225,000 by 1994. The plan has resulted in the first IBM layoffs since the company was founded in 1914 . . .

"It's something we must do to stay competitive," spokesman Stephen Cole said.

From the New York Times
March 11, 1994

The chairman and chief executive of the IBM Corporation, Louis V. Gerstner, Jr., has earned $7.71 million in salary, bonuses and other cash compensation since he joined IBM in March.

Mr. Gerstner, 52, also received stock options that could be worth up to $38.2 million. . .

He is to receive a total of $8.5 million for his last 12 months of service, a spokesman for IBM said.

to college. Health problems became a major fear because people no longer had the protection and peace of mind that came with company-sponsored medical benefits. Without the security of a pension, retirement became a source of financial anxiety and stress rather than a time to enjoy the fruits of a lifetime's worth of labor.

While their own lives were falling apart, these same workers saw that their employers' betrayal of loyalty to them was paying very handsome dividends to CEOs and shareholders. On the same day that IBM announced it was going to lay off more workers, the *New York Times* reported that Lou Gerstner, Jr., IBM's chairman and CEO, was receiving $8.5 million for the sterling job he had done for the company the previous year.

To many, it seemed Gerstner was actually getting a bonus for having the stomach to turn his company's loyal employees out on the streets. The fact is, IBM was running the risk of going out of business and if it wasn't for Gerstner, might well have done so. But, this provided little comfort for those who were put "out of business" when their jobs were cut.

Gerstner wasn't alone in the headlines. The infamous poster boy for downsizing became a West Point graduate named Albert Dunlap. Dunlap raised downsizing to such proportions that he was dubbed "Rambo in Pinstripes" or "Chainsaw Al" by the media. He was called far worse by those he let go.

Al Dunlap took over Scott Paper in April of 1994. The company had been teetering on the brink of collapse for several years. The former CEO had already downsized 8,300 workers over the past three years, but that was nothing compared to what Al had planned.

Al walked in the door at Scott Paper and promptly dismissed 10 of the top 11 executives at the company. That same year, Al eliminated 11,200 jobs or about one third of the total workforce so that the company could "survive."

In what many people considered a bitter irony, Dunlap then sold the company to its chief competitor, Lily Tulip, for $7 billion in stock. Old "Chainsaw," after only a year on the job, walked away from the deal $100 million richer!

But Al wasn't finished yet. In late 1996, word came that Al Dunlap was moving his "slash and burn" show to Sunbeam Corporation.

His first actions at Sunbeam included:

- Shutting all six corporate headquarters and replanting them into 50,000 square feet in Delray Beach, Florida;

- Shrinking the number of factories from 26 to 8 and the number of warehouses from 61 to 24;

- Firing 3,000 of 12,000 Sunbeam employees, leaving 9,000 workers, one third of whom worked for business divisions that were later sold off.

For Dunlap and leaders like him, all of these actions were aimed at achieving only one result: increase shareholder value (i.e., make the price of stock go higher). Stock price became then – and is now – the major measure by which corporate productivity and value are gauged. Massive layoffs are one of the easiest and fastest ways to make a company's stock price jump.

In 1993, Boeing, IBM and United Technologies all announced they were laying off employees by the tens of thousands. Wall Street applauded and by the end of the year, these companies were rewarded with increases in stock value of 30% or more.

What did not make the headlines, however, was that in many cases, the stock prices for many of these companies eventually sank back below their original levels.

Al Dunlap had a similar impact on shareholder value with his strategies at Sunbeam.

The responsibility of the
CEO is to deliver
shareholder value.

Period.

It's the shareholders
who own the corporation.
They take all the risk.

– Al Dunlap
Does America Still Work, 1996

Al Dunlap Joins Sunbeam

July 18, 1996

Al Dunlap elected Chairman/CEO

Sunbeam stock opens at $12.50

Stock surges to $18.50 overnight

– "Chainsaw" Al cuts 12,000 jobs at Sunbeam –

March 4, 1998

Sunbeam stock hits a high of $53.00

The real kicker, though, is this. Recent reports show that Sunbeam and other companies overdid a good thing. Some downsizing may have been necessary in order to make these companies effective and efficient. The problem was that many companies cut, not with a scalpel, but with a meat cleaver, lopping off so many employees that the companies couldn't operate effectively. And, stock prices continued to slide downward after their early post-layoff highs. Sunbeam learned this lesson all to well, as did many other companies.

The Demise of Sunbeam

June 16, 1998

Due to poor performance (stock value had been falling for several months) and a disagreement with Sunbeam's board

Al Dunlap is ousted from the company

June 19, 1998

Sunbeam stock is down to $11.25

November 19, 1999	
	Sunbeam stock drops to $5.00
September 22, 2000	
	Sunbeam stock is at $1.75
February 1, 2001	
	Sunbeam stock at $.51 New York Stock Exchange threatens to remove Sunbeam from its listing
February 7, 2001	
	Sunbeam files for bankruptcy

Sunbeam paid a heavy price for its slash and burn leadership and they weren't alone. However, while employees and companies suffered, downsizing gurus grew conspicuously richer. Al Dunlap may have been fired from Sunbeam, but he was far from being out on the street looking for his next meal. His take-no-prisoners approach had made him millions. In fact, while severance packages for rank-and-file employees have shrunk over the years – if they are offered at all – CEOs are getting bulging severance packages, even if they've been fired for poor performance on the job.

So, let's look again at downsizing from the perspective of the employee and the idea that "If you work hard and take care of the company, the company will take care of you."

- Today, employees are still expected to work hard for the company but job security has become a myth.

- Employees and the public see that a company's top priority, at any price, is the bottom line. As a result, individual jobs are willingly sacrificed on the altar of shareholder value.

- Most employees are alienated from top management and don't trust corporate leaders to protect them, their jobs, or their future.

Even people lucky enough not to have been laid off or threatened by downsizing themselves at least of know someone who has. The media has also made sure we all know about the battering people's lives have taken after they've been laid off. We also know that companies frequently see a big pop in the price of their stock (at least in the short term) whenever they announce big layoffs. With this in mind, it is safe to say that almost all employees, regardless of the company they work for, have lost their faith that the company they work for will "take care of them" – especially when stock prices are at risk.

But, let us not forget that downsizing was only one of the two strategies organizations embraced to improve their performance. While many companies were implementing their downsizing programs, another strategy was also in play – merger & acquisition. Some thought if they couldn't "shrink" their way to bigger profits, they could "transact" their way there through merger and acquisition deals. This dose of corporate medicine was even harder for many employees to swallow.

Transacting for Success

The desire to increase stock price also had companies courting each other through merger and acquisition to produce "economies of scale." They believed that by marrying two or more organizations together, they could pool resources and make a stronger and more profitable organization. This strategy is still going strong. Huge deals are announced almost daily. For example, in 1999, America Online unveiled 21 M&A deals alone. Then, in late 2000, came the announcement of AOL's merger with Time Warner – the largest merger ever designed.

The goal of these M&A deals is quite simple. Companies are constantly battling to minimize competition and improve performance – and, of course, bump up shareholder value. If two (or more) companies band together, they can cut costs by shedding duplicate divisions, pooling their resources, and capturing an even larger piece of the market.

And, in case you missed it, getting rid of duplicate divisions also entails eliminating jobs. A newly merged company doesn't need 3,000 salespeople when only 1,000 are required to sell the company's products or 40 division heads when 20 will do the trick. For employees in both companies, a merger or acquisition guarantees that layoffs are on the horizon.

However, companies are just beginning to realize that mergers and acquisitions aren't just a simple mater of slapping two organizations together, dumping the excess and then rolling in huge new profits. Merger announcements may make headlines but the failures don't get near as much attention. Few people are aware that the collapse of an attempted merger is commonplace, and the resulting slide of stock value is often dramatic and, in some cases, devastating.

- A merger between AT&T and NCR was initially considered a very lucrative deal. However, "cultural/employee issues" resulted in AT&T selling NCR in 1997. The failure cost AT&T more than $3 billion and NCR half its market value.

- The American Home Products and Monsanto merger was called off after five months due to cultural differences. Monsanto's shares lost 27% of their value and AHP lost 10%.

- A post-merger performance study of 150 companies that had merged between 1990 and 1995 found that fully half of the mergers had failed. Their stockholder returns lagged behind similar companies during the same three-year period. The culprits were almost always conflicting corporate cultures and poor communication with employees.

The biggest problem looming over M&A deals is that top management in both companies are usually so busy working out all the financial aspects of the deal, they forget about people. They fail to realize that in order to reap the rewards they envision for a merger, they must first get their employees motivated and focused on doing what needs to be done to make the deal a reality.

Mergers are periods of enormous transition and uncertainty for employees. Just the threat of being laid off, relocated, or any number of other unpleasant consequences makes staying focused on the job very tough for most workers. Employees are left to wonder how the merger will alter their lives.

- What will be the rules of the game for getting and keeping a job in the newly fused organization?

- Will they even have a job when the merger is complete?

In essence, coming to work becomes an exercise in trying to keep your job rather than doing your job.

Many companies have found themselves unable to capture the synergy and financial advantage that made a M&A deal attractive in the first place. They failed to consider the impact of the transition on employees. In M&A deals, maintaining performance is key. Successful M&A deals require that everyone in the organization work together and focus on maximizing results. Considering how companies have been treating their employees, it shouldn't be any wonder that many come in each day doing just enough to get by.

Corporate America Rebounds

To be fair, downsizing and M&A's did, in many cases, have an upside. American companies made a major comeback, standing once again atop the global corporate marketplace. On July 7, 1997, *Business Week* reflected just how strong American industry's bounce back had been.

- The U.S. had once again snared over half (56 to be exact) of the top 100 spots on the most highly valued corporations – up from only 24 in 1995. The list is worldwide.

- Of the top 10 most-highly-valued global companies, seven were U.S. based organizations.

The news has stayed good. In another global competitiveness report issued in 1998, the U.S. once again ranked number one on both technology and research.

Despite the wrenching effects of downsizing and M&A activity on their employees, many of the companies who did downsize or merge made their way back to top positions on the global playing field. But strangely, a return to preeminence has not meant that corporations have stopped shedding workers or looking to reposition themselves through merger & acquisition. In fact, the opposite seems to be true.

The Shrinking And Transacting Continues

Life for employees would be much different if America's return to a position of strength in the global economy meant that companies were taking a break from laying off bunches of people or that M&A activity had paused to take a breath. That hasn't happened. If anything, both downsizing and M&A trends have increased in the 1990's and are likely to continue to increase into the foreseeable future.

Layoffs From 1996-2000 (in millions)

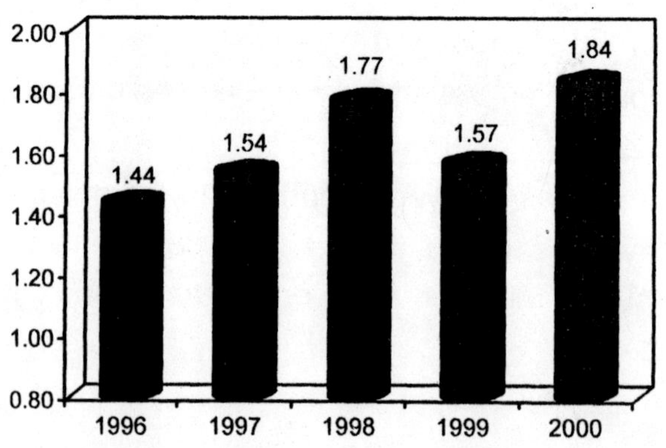

Source: US Bureau of Labor Statistics, 2001

As the chart illustrates, massive layoff trends have been booming, except for a tiny drop in 1999. This fact bodes ill for many employees, who can expect that the new millennium will result in even more layoff threats to their jobs. In fact, December 2000 topped the layoff list, generating the highest number of job cut announcements ever reported for a single month – a total of 133,713. This was only the fourth time since 1993 that the number of job cuts rose higher than 100,000 for a single month.

In the year 2001, the boom in layoffs continued. The first half of the year alone was estimated to eliminate some 777,362 jobs, compared with 613,960 in all of last year.

- DaimlerChrysler announces plans to drop more than 25,000 of its employees.

- America Online says it will shrink its workforce by one third.

- General Electric announces it will lay off more than 75,000 workers worldwide by 2002.

The trend is unmistakable. Companies will continue to use the meat axe on their payrolls in order to boost their stock price. The result is that a majority of employees will perpetually – and rightfully – be in fear of losing their jobs.

Mergers and acquisitions show the same trend. From 1970-1996, the number of deals in the U.S. hovered at around 5,000 a year. In 1997, the number skyrocketed 230% to over 11,000 deals in one year, ushering in a new era for merger mania.

Number of M&A Deals in the U.S. and Their Projected Value

Year	No. of Transactions	Total Value
1970	5,152	$16.4 billion
↓	↓ ↓ ↓	↓ ↓
1996	4,790	$369 billion
1997	11,029	$908 Billion
1998	11,400	$1.2 trillion
1999	9,192	$1.7 trillion
2000	10,013	$1.9 trillion

And, while we have featured data and trends primarily from the U.S., don't think the rest of the world is far behind. True, the U.S. has relied most heavily on slash and burn strategies over the years, but more and more, companies across the globe are playing at merging their power and resources to better compete in competitive markets.

In 1985, out of the global total of M&A's for that year, the U.S. was responsible for the lion's share of these deals by the tune of 83%. However, in 2000, with the total number and value of deals increasingly on the rise, the U.S. could only claim just over 50% of those M&A's.

The big question is whether these mergers and acquisitions, be they in the U.S. or elsewhere, can live up to their billing. Don't bet on it.

There are some new, very sinister buzzwords emerging in the global marketplace. For example, in Europe, organizational ***demergers*** and ***disposals*** are gaining in popularity. While many organizations are still cruising the corporate bars looking for their perfect mate(s), others have found that what they had hoped to be profit-making marriages are falling apart and they are choosing to file for "divorce." While demergers/disposals aren't grabbing top headlines at the moment, if economic trends take a downturn, they could very well increase dramatically. And, if mergers are tough on employees, imagine the turmoil engendered by a "demerger" or "disposal."

In a world where corporate strategies of coupling companies, undoing them again, and in both cases, dumping employees, are firmly entrenched in boardroom arsenals, employees will continue to be the ones hammered the hardest. Stockholders may have a happier smile on their faces (at least for the short term), but that satisfaction is at the expense of people who have either already lost their jobs or who live in constant fear of losing them.

It's common sense that people who are preoccupied with the potential loss of the livelihood – or people who have had their corporate loyalty betrayed before – can't and won't focus 100% of their energy, initiative and creativity on the job at hand. Leaders at every level of organizations will be faced with the stark reality of trying to squeeze more and more productivity from people who may be more and more focused on doing everything but their job. The breach of the workplace contract...

If you work hard and take care of the company, the company will take care of you.

...has created a workforce that goes to work on a crumbling foundation of mistrust, distrust or no trust.

Leaders will now have to face the new employee credo:

Treat me badly, and I'll get even. I'll give you less work, sloppier work or I may just not come in again – ever.

The Impact Of The Broken Contract

Why was the workplace contract so valuable? Why was it such an integral part of the relationship between companies and their employees? Why should everyone, from CEO to front-line supervisor, worry that they are managing people who no longer believe that "If you work hard and take care of the company, the company will take care of you?"

In hindsight, the workplace contract was a company's greatest asset. Why? Because the old workplace contract was based on a simple principle that most people were taught by their parents. You get what you give and if you treat people right, they'll treat you right. That's **Equity**.

How does the principle of Equity function in the workplace? Employees give the company hard work and loyalty; in return, they expect pay, job security, and eventually, some kind of retirement security. We call this Give-to-Get ratio the **Equity Equation**. The balance between what we give and what we get is at the heart of human behavior in and out of the workplace. Without the old workplace contract...

If you work hard and take care of the company,
the company will take care of you.

...employees feel that what they give to their company far exceeds what they get in return. The threat of layoffs, the neglect produced by management's obsession with boosting shareholder value, and the battering employees get from constant change (mergers, layoffs or otherwise), means that the motivation employees had to excel at their work has vanished like snow in summer sunshine. Without this motivation, it is difficult for leaders to secure high performance from their teams.

The Age Of Free Agency In The Workplace

When companies started dumping hundreds of thousands of employees from their payrolls, a new era was born – the Age of Free Agency. It was a world most were not prepared for. After years of working under the old workplace contract and the security it provided, most people were ill prepared to start working as free agents.

Who and what are free agents? Basically, they're workers who have no fixed allegiance to any one company. They hop from organization to organization, project to project and opportunity to opportunity. They work for one corporation, move on to another company (maybe even the competitor of the first one), then slide right back to the first company – if the price is right. Free agents have been called "boomerang employees," "free-lancers," "consultants," etc.

Free agents are entrepreneurs with a twist. They don't start projects. Instead they promote and market their individual skills and talents to companies to obtain work on existing or future projects. These workers keep their eyes on the horizon, looking for their next big opportunity wherever it may be, instead of roosting in one particular organization and confining their search to whatever that corporation has available.

Free agents are very similar to actors. Actors look for roles which suit them. They audition for a part and if they have the most talent, or the right connections, they are cast. Then, they take on that role until the play's run or the movie's filming are finished. When that is over, they move on to the next role.

Free agents operate by similar rules. However, the work life of a free agent (or actor) is never secure. There is no guarantee that they will find more work after their current project is done. But, if they are talented and have skills that are in demand, free agents can ask for (and usually receive) much more in terms of money and resources than their single-company counterparts. Free agents have much more control over how, where and when they do their work than long-term, established corporate employees.

The shift from the security of being a loyal employee to being a free agent can be dramatic, and traumatic, for workers. However, many have adapted quickly and well. They have the added advantage of having a strong marketing and support network to make finding and securing great opportunities easier for them. Talent auction websites like freeagent.com, elance,com, bid4geeks.com, brainbid.com and monster.com, have opened up a whole new world for free agents seeking their livelihoods.

On these sites, organizations can sculpt project profiles that list what money and time parameters, reporting relationships, etc. they are willing to offer. In return, free agents carve their own profiles spelling out their skills, how much money they want, preferred work locations, availability, etc. When the auction goes "live," organizations usually end up bidding for free agents instead of the other way around. The free agent then accepts or rejects the bid. Almost everything becomes negotiable.

Free agent workers have far more control over their Equity Equation in their jobs because they spell out what they will give and what they will get from their work relationships.

The Dilemma For Today's Manager/Leader

After so many years of downsizing, merger and acquisition, when leaders dictated whether a worker would still have a job with the company the next day, today's leader is trying to motivate two very different groups of workers. On the one hand, you have employees who feel like they are standing on the gallows trap door with a noose around their neck. They're just waiting for the company to pull the handle and let the trap door fly open thereby killing their employment with that company. These employees work well enough – just enough so they won't get fired – but they're certainly not interested in giving their best performance in a job where they are not valued or appreciated. Especially if that job might not be there tomorrow.

On the other hand, some of the very best performers a leader has may decide that they can become free agents. Even if the company pays them well, these employees can, and very well might, defect to the competition if they get a better offer. If these employees walk out the door, then a leader must also watch their talent and knowledge leave with them. It's a huge loss for the company, and, if you are their leader, it's a blow to you as well.

The old workplace contract:

If you work hard and take care of the company,
the company will take care of you

in most companies is dead. The result is that the Equity Equation has become lopsided in favor of organizations. So, how do you lead and manage in this new environment?

If you want to compete effectively, you have to rebalance the Equity Equation for your employees. You must become a Give-to-Get Leader and pay your employees their long overdue Hidden Paycheck. The Hidden Paycheck is not about money. You can't really hold it in your hands. However, in many cases, it's worth a lot more to your employees than cash.

In the next few chapters, you'll see what the Hidden Paycheck is, how it operates, and you can deploy it so you and your company can get winning performance and profits.

Give naught, get same.

Give much, get same.

– Malcolm Forbes

Chapter 3
The Equity Equation: Charlie's Story

A few years ago, we were flying from Atlanta to Pittsburgh. Across the aisle was seated a man who looked to be about sixty years old. His wavy hair was graying, and he was wearing a finely tailored suit. Despite his distinguished and elegant appearance, he was slumped in his seat, the wrinkles in his face were deeply etched, and the bags under his eyes almost sagged under their weight. He looked unusually troubled and tired.

Somehow we struck up a conversation. He said his name was Charlie. As a business consultant with a major consulting firm, Charlie had worked alongside upper management in numerous high-level organizations around the world. He was at the top of his game and on the top rung of his profession. By most standards, he was enormously successful.

Charlie asked where we were going and what we were doing there. We told him that we were giving a seminar in Toronto. The topic, we told him: "The Equity Equation: After All I've Done for You..." Charlie, looking introspective, repeated the title aloud.

"That's the story of my life," he said, quietly. And for the next hour, as strangers on an airplane will do, he told us his story.

Charlie's Wife

Charlie talked about his relationship with his former wife. He freely admitted he traveled a lot, was often absent on weekends and sometimes forgot a birthday or anniversary. But he'd worked hard at his job and he had made many important contributions to his marriage. He'd brought home a large paycheck that financed a luxury home complete with a private wine cellar. He and his wife occasionally vacationed at exotic getaways where usually only the rich and famous went.

Imagine Charlie's astonishment when he returned home from a business trip one Friday evening to find that his wife had moved out. At the divorce hearing, Charlie learned for the first time that his wife of 27 years hadn't wanted more of his money, just more of his time.

Charlie's Daughter

Charlie also talked about the significant contributions he'd made to the relationship with his daughter. He'd always returned from his travels with special gifts for her. He reveled in the ecstatic look on her face as she peeled the wrappings off the box.

Of course, he sometimes felt guilty because he was absent so much from his daughter's life, but he knew he was earning money enough to give her a fine education at one of the best schools. When the time came, she did indeed attend a rather expensive college. Charlie thought he had prepared for the cost of college years. However, the more money he sent his daughter, the more she seemed to want. His burden became almost crushing when she moved out of her $325-a-semester dorm room and into a $550-a-month apartment, while instructing the landlord to ship the bill for rent to ever-obliging Charlie.

But she did graduate, and he attended her graduation with tears in his eyes – not because he was thrilled that she had finally received her degree after five and a half years, but because he was thinking about the thousands of dollars he still owed for her education.

When we asked how his daughter was doing now, he slumped in his seat and spoke very softly.

"I really don't know," he whispered, his eyes downcast. "I haven't seen or talked to her in more than three years."

Charlie's Dog

As part of his divorce settlement, Charlie and his ex-wife sold their home and split the proceeds. He rented an apartment and bought a dog for $600. Of course, that price was just the beginning. There were trips to the veterinarian, who handed Charlie bills high enough to make him wish for a canine HMO. And there were other expenses, such as obedience training and pet-sitters for when he was out of town, plus numerous additional bills.

Charlie paid them all, feeling that at least he had a warm and friendly creature to come home to. Those good feelings ended one night when Charlie returned home from a business trip. As he opened the door, Charlie's $600 dog zoomed across the room and sank its teeth into Charlie's leg. Charlie took the dog to the pound the next day.

Charlie's Job

As our plane landed in Pittsburgh, we asked Charlie where he was headed.

"I'm checking into a psychiatric hospital," he said, his voice low so that the other passengers couldn't hear him. "After all I've done for my company, my bosses tell me I'm burning out. So, they forced me to take a leave of absence and come to this nuthouse."

Charlie paused a second, then sharply drew in his breath. "I hope the shrinks here know what they're doin'. If I don't snap out of this depression, the company may toss me out on the street."

Charlie explained that he couldn't afford that. Like a lot of other executives, part of his pay had been in stock options. Now, though, the company's prospects had sunk pretty low. Bad planning and worse management, combined with a rapidly deteriorating stock market, meant his stocks had lost much of their value. His net worth had sunk from $1 million to less than $150,000 in 18 months.

At age sixty, Charlie was alone and feeling abandoned, bewildered by a life once full of promising relationships, none of which seemed to be working out. We could well understand why the expression, "After all I've done for you..." rang such bells for him.

Sadly, though Charlie is lonely, he's far from alone.

Consider ...Each day across this country 13,000 people say "I do." At the same time, more than 6,700 people are asking a court to bury their marriages. That fact means 52% of all marriages end in divorce – a bit more than one out of two. And those are just the official statistics. There are uncounted numbers of couples who long ago divorced each other emotionally but still live together.

Consider...each day across this country, it is estimated that 50,000 people quit their jobs. Some are moving to better jobs. Many are not. And these statistics ignore still other people who have also "quit" their jobs but keep coming to work doing just enough to collect their paychecks. In fact, in a recent survey of workers across the United States, nearly 85% said that they could work harder on the job. More than half claimed they could double their effectiveness "if I wanted to."

We hope you don't fall into one of these statistical categories. We also hope that you don't have a lot in common with Charlie. But many people do and the real tragedy is that:

- It's not our intentions that cause problems in relationships. Most of us want to have satisfying and strong relationships both at work and at home.

- It's not that we don't try to maintain healthy relationships. We spend untold hours thinking about, worrying over, and seeking advice about our work and personal relationships.

- It's what we *don't know* that causes us to do what we should not do... and not do what we should do to have more productive and more satisfying relationships in life.

As you read the following pages, you'll come to a new understanding of why people act and react the way they do, especially in their work relationships. As you'll see, the single most powerful principle in managing healthy relationships – both in and out of work – is what we call the **Equity Equation**. Essentially, it means that you get what you give. Our goal here is to offer strategies that you, as a leader, can put to work for you, giving you more effective and productive relationships with your employees, while getting high performance and profitability in return. These strategies, in combination, make up **The Hidden Paycheck**.

Be warned, the most difficult realization you will have to make is that your intentions, your effort, or the amount of time you contribute to your work relationships are not what count. Instead, it is how other people "perceive" your actions and other contributions. In the case of workplace relationships, "Equity" is definitely in the eye of the beholder.

N	O	T	E
V	E	R	Y
O	N	E	W
I	L	L	G
E	T	E	Q
U	I	T	Y

(If you have trouble decoding the message, check the note at the bottom of the page for the answer)

In order to explain how the Equity Equation works, we will do the following:

- First, we'll explore what elements comprise the Equity Equation and what its impact is on human relationships.

- Second, we'll show you why your employees might not understand or appreciate your contributions in your relationship with them.

** Again, the secret to this little riddle is to read the first word as "not." The message then quickly reads, "Not everyone will get equity."*

- Third, we'll identify some specific reasons work relationships can be tough to manage and how many companies, led by their own leaders, lean toward doing exactly the wrong things with exactly the right intentions.

- Finally, we'll illustrate how you can begin using the Hidden Paycheck to achieve more productive and satisfying relationships with your employees. You'll like the results you get in return.

Give me that which
I want...

...and you shall have
that which you want.

– Adam Smith

Chapter 4
The Three Laws of Equity

The flight where we met Charlie was more eventful than we knew. While we were waiting at a curb for our bags to be checked, we observed the people ahead of us. Most of them would hand the skycap a couple of bucks and asked him to make sure their bags got on the right plane.

The person directly in front of us, however, took an entirely different approach. He didn't offer the skycap a tip, but he did sternly lecture the skycap about taking special care of his two bags. He swore loudly when one of his bags tipped over accidentally, then angrily stalked off toward his gate.

As we stepped up to take our turn, the skycap's broad smile caught our attention.

"I don't understand," I told him. "How are you able to keep smiling when you sometimes have to deal with such difficult people?"

"What do you mean?" he asked.

"That fellow who just swore at you," I replied.

The skycap smiled again. "Oh, that dude? People like him are easy. You see, he's heading for L.A., but his bags are going to Detroit!"

In a nutshell, this incident sums up the flip side of what happens when people don't perceive equity in a relationship. They find a way to even the score.

People **give** to **get**. Seems pretty simple, doesn't it? Your parents probably told you a version of the same thing. They might put it, "Treat people nicely and they'll treat you nicely," or something similar.

They were right. You'll see evidence of this principle at work all around you. When you open a door for someone, you expect a simple thanks, a smile, maybe both, in return. On a business level, you might expect a greater level of commitment from employees after you've given them a bonus.

At work, many of us have, at one time or another, mumbled (if only to ourselves), "I don't get PAID enough to put up with this!" This statement is a simple outward expression of an inner feeling, the feeling that whatever you're giving in your corporate relationship is more than what you're getting, and you don't like getting the short end of the stick. You feel shortchanged.

Why? Because beneath that feeling lurks the most potent principle of human behavior: the **Equity Equation**.

The Equity Equation has a rich history in philosophy, economics, anthropology, and psychology. In fact, the notion of equity was first set forth more than two thousand years ago. In his *Nicomachean Ethics*,

Aristotle left little doubt that what people give and get is at the core of human relationships.

The very existence of the state depends on reciprocity... It is exchange that binds men together.

Nothing in the give-to-get principle Aristotle set forward over 20 centuries ago has changed. Consider our skycap. Whether he knew it or not, he was reacting to an imbalance in his Equity Equation. When faced with a guy who was rude, condescending and who didn't even offer him a tip, the skycap "evened the equity score" by making sure the man's bags didn't get to the correct destination.

As leaders, while we might smile at the skycap's story, we need to consider the fact that our employees might be sending our bags to the wrong destination every day in ways that we are frequently not aware of.

It is the Equity Equation and the relationship between give-to-get that is at the heart of human behavior – both at home and at work.

If you give enough people what they want, eventually, you will get what you want.

– Truett Cathy, *President*
Chick-fil-A, Inc.

The very existence of the state depends on reciprocity . . .

It is exchange that binds men together.

– Aristotle
Nicomachean Ethics
350 B.C.

The Equity Equation And Relationships

As leaders, we want employees to be productive and committed. But we are often disappointed when they arrive late for work, take extended breaks and lunch hours, and call in sick even though we're sure that they're not. We wonder why they sometimes pad their expense accounts, work on personal projects during work hours, take company property home for their personal use, and even commit acts of sabotage. And we feel especially betrayed when they suddenly quit their jobs and go to work for another company – especially when it is our major competitor.

But, hold on. Before leaders, including you, start blaming the people working for their lack of loyalty, they might first want to try looking in the mirror. Remember, people give to get. So, if you aren't getting what you need from a relationship, then chances are you're not giving either– at least not the right things.

Let's try a short exercise. Think about one important work relationship you have – with a subordinate, co-worker, boss, organization, etc.

On the left-hand side of the work area on the next page, draw up a list of all the contributions you make to this relationship – what you are giving. If it's with your employees, you might be providing them with pay, job security, professional development opportunities, etc.

What I Give	What I Get

Make your list as lengthy as you can. Notice that this list is titled "What I Give."

On the right-hand side of the work area, make a second list of "What I Get." Write down all the benefits that you are receiving from your relationship. Loyalty? Support? Hard work? Creativity? Talent? Make this lengthy, too, if you can.

No item is too big or too small. For both lists, do not, repeat, do not, number the items. Just list them.

Now sit back and compare your two lists. Don't count the number of items on each one. Some things are more important than others. And you've probably left some items off both lists. Instead, answer this simple question:

Considering all that you give to your relationship versus all that you're getting from it, who is getting the better deal?

Choose one from the following three options:

- ❑ I'm getting the better deal.
- ❑ We're getting an equally good deal.
- ❑ The other person is getting a better deal

Now, let's consider your answer in terms of the three Laws of Equity.

Equity Law I

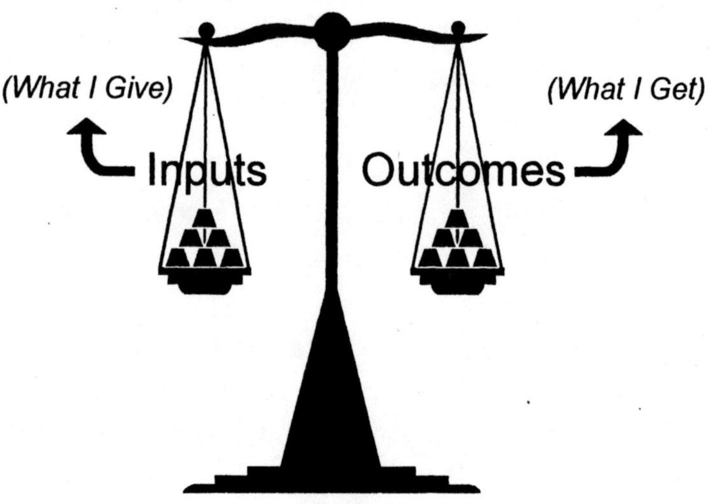

People Give To Get

People evaluate relationships by comparing what they give to a relationship with what they get from it.

Equity Law I: People Give To Get

People evaluate their relationships by comparing what they give to a relationship with what they get from it.

What you contribute to relationships ("What I Give") we call Inputs. What you receive in return ("What I Get") we called Outcomes or payoffs. Moments ago when you compared what you gave to your work relationship and what you got from it, you were evaluating your Inputs versus your Outcomes. You made a conscious attempt to calculate your give-to-get ratio for this particular relationship, but most of the time, probably without even realizing it, you have made similar comparisons subconsciously. And not just with this specific relationship. You are processing your Equity Equation in all relationships, all the time.

Picture a tiny computer-like gizmo in the back of your mind. This computer tracks what you put into relationships and what you get back. This computer switches on when you first pop into the world, and it shuts down only when you close your eyes for the last time. You can't turn it off. It keeps on going, categorizing new Inputs and Outcomes, reprioritizing their importance, and sometimes removing them completely. All the time this computer is functioning, it's calculating and recalculating your **Equity Score**.

Who Has Equity In The Workplace?

	Managers	Non Managers
Feel over-rewarded	13%	7%
Feel equitably rewarded	34%	10%
Feel under-rewarded	53%	83%

Usually this computer gizmo is humming along so quietly you don't even know it's operating. But if Inputs and Outcomes get too far out of balance, then it will let you know in a hurry that your Equity Score is too lopsided one way or another.

So, what's your Equity Score for the relationship you were just thinking about? If your answer was, "I'm getting the better deal," then you may be Over-Rewarded in this relationship.

If your answer was, "We are getting an equally good deal," then your Inputs are fairly equal to your Outcomes and your Equity Equation is in balance.

But, if your answer was, "The other person is getting a better deal," then you may be Under-Rewarded (you aren't getting enough from the relationship because your Inputs are getting too far ahead of your Outcomes).

Now, if the relationship you were evaluating was with a superior or with your organization as a whole and you feel as though you're giving a lot more than you're getting – you are in the vast majority.

How do we know? During the last few years, we've asked several thousand people, both managers and hourly workers, in some of America's largest corporations to tell us who's getting the better deal – they or the organization they work for. The chart to the left lists the troubling results.

As you can see, over half of the managers in the organizations we surveyed feel Under-Rewarded (they think their organization is getting the better deal). What's perhaps even more troubling is that more than 80% of non-managers feel that their employer is getting the better deal.

Psychologists don't know how people make the actual comparison between what they give and what they get from relationships. Some psychologists think we compare ourselves to someone in a position or situation similar to our own.

For example, someone might feel underpaid for the amount of work done because a coworker does less work but gets paid the same salary. Or someone might feel Under-Rewarded if they are passed over for promotion and someone else who has fewer years experience with the company receives the position instead.

Others think people compare their Inputs and Outcomes against a standard that experiences earlier in life have etched into their mind. For example, people who have been married more than once might gauge Inputs and Outcomes in their current marriage by what they gave (or didn't give) and got (or didn't get) in their previous marriage(s).

Or maybe people feel Under-Rewarded for their work because an earlier job paid just as well as the one they currently have, but the work is much harder, the hours are longer, or there's some other factor which doesn't stack up favorably.

A third possibility is that people compare their Inputs and Outcomes to what the other person in the relationship seems to be giving and getting. So, you yourself might feel you're getting the better deal if the other person is putting more time and effort into your relationship, but you're giving that person a lot less in return.

All of which leads us to Equity Law II.

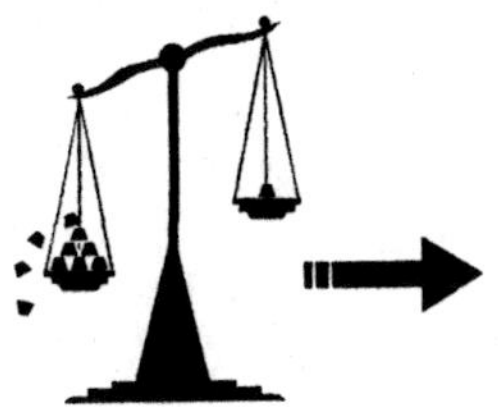

Equity Law II

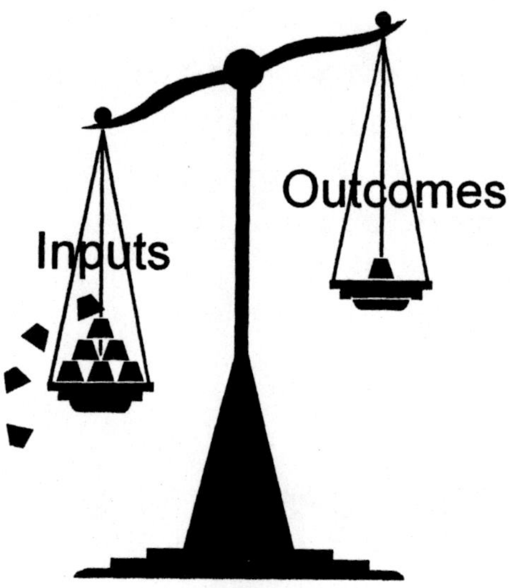

Inequity Creates Stress

When what people give to a relationship does not equal what they get from it, they feel stress.

The Secret of
THE HIDDEN PAYCHECK

Equity Law II: Inequity Creates Stress

When what people give to a relationship does not equal what they get from it, they feel stress.

While nobody seems to know the basis for how people make comparisons between Inputs and Outcomes, it's clear that people do make these comparisons. These calculations produce one of three feelings:

- **Over-Rewarded:** Getting more than they're giving
- **Equitably Rewarded:** Getting as good as they're giving
- **Under-Rewarded:** Getting less than they're giving

You also now know that, typically, many people in organizations feel they're getting less than they're giving – often, a lot less. And, of course, you know how you feel about the particular relationship you evaluated a little bit earlier.

But it's not just how people feel about these relationships, it's how they react to those feelings. The stress you feel over inequitable relationships – yes, even the ones where you've got the better deal – depends on who feels they're being cheated. People who are getting more than they're giving tend to feel ***guilt***. People who are giving more than they're getting often experience ***resentment***.

The Guilt of Over-Reward

Have you ever received too much change after a purchase in a department store, but you didn't realize it until you were in the car? Have you received a lavish gift from a friend for whom you did a very small favor? If so, then you know how it feels to be Over-Rewarded.

Sometimes, the guilt of Over-Reward can be utilized against us in some very ingenious ways. For example:

- Companies selling vacation properties like to use the ploy of offering prospects three "grand prizes" in a special drawing. The only obligation for having won is to visit the property to pick up the prize. If that winner were you, wouldn't you feel a little guilty if you didn't at least listen to a sales pitch on the property while you were there?

- Charitable organizations sometimes send stamps, address labels or other small gifts. All they want is a donation in return. Some of us ignore that plea, but the guilt of being Over-Rewarded will compel some of us to send money, even though we didn't ask for the gift in the first place. Others will give the gift away or actually throw it out to banish the feeling of Over-Reward.

- Some organizations send surveys with a request that you fill them out. Most of these surveys wind up in the trashcan. Other organizations send a half dollar or a dollar with the survey. Many of these surveys are completed and returned. In fact, an executive who conducts surveys of retail storeowners told us about one retailer who returned his uncompleted survey, the dollar, and a letter of apology for not having the time to complete the survey. The survey would have taken no more than two minutes to complete. We wonder how long it took the retailer to write his letter.

Two university professors once shared what has become our favorite example of Over-Reward. Several years ago, as part of a research project, the professors sent out holiday greeting cards to 528 total strangers. More than one hundred of their surprised recipients of the holiday greeting responded with either a card of their own, or an entire letter.

While most of the returning cards contained only a signature, many others included handwritten notes about their family or recalling old friendships with these two professors. Some people even included pictures of their families, pets, and friends. Only six people who sent back cards said that they couldn't remember the professors and asked for more information!

The reason the professors got so many responses is that people do try to keep relationships balanced evenly, and the guilt of being Over-Rewarded causes some people to respond in unexpected ways.

The Resentment of Under-Reward

The way people respond to feeling guilty about being Over-Rewarded can be odd, even funny. But it's the flip side of the give-to-get stress spectrum leaders have to worry about. When people feel the resentment of being Under-Rewarded, watch out!

Remember that 53% of managers and 83% of non-managers feel Under-Rewarded in their relationships with their organizations. Some people are probably only mildly irritated by this situation. Others are genuinely angry. In fact, many of the Under-Rewarded people in these organizations report that they are significantly less satisfied in their jobs than their Equitably Rewarded counterparts.

People who are Over-Rewarded may feel guilty, but when people are frustrated and angry because they are giving more than they are getting, that feeling compels them to react predictably, decisively, and, often, destructively.

This leads us to the final Equity Law.

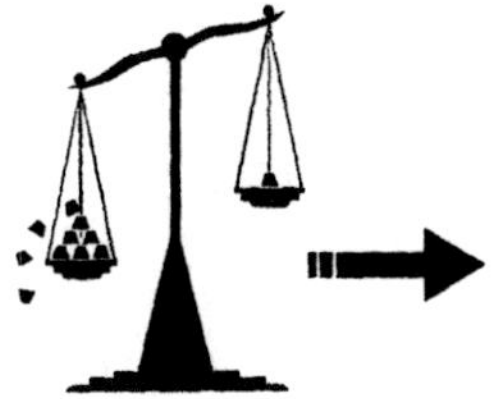

Equity Law III

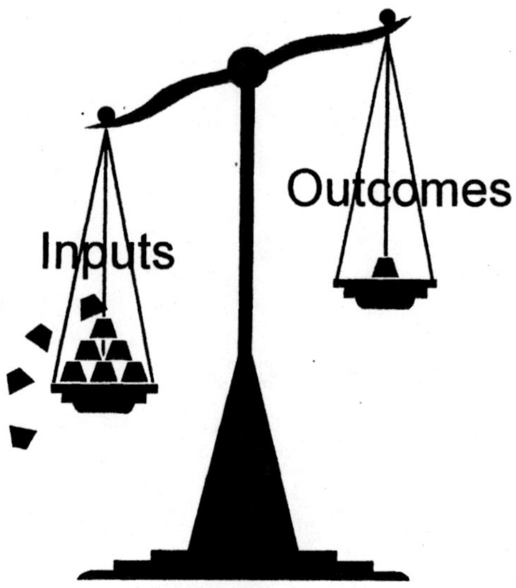

People Will Attempt To Restore Equity

People who feel stress in relationships because they give more than they get will engage in behaviors to restore equity.

Equity Law III: People Will Attempt To Restore Equity

People who feel stress in relationships because they give more than they get will engage in behaviors to restore equity.

Remember the expression we have all mumbled (or shouted) at one time or another, "I'm not *PAID* enough for this!" This utterance says, "I'm not getting the Outputs I need from our work relationship" and is a huge warning sign that an employee feels badly Under-Rewarded. When people feel the resentment of being Under-Rewarded, they will try to restore the balance of equity in one of three ways.

1. People Will Reduce Inputs

2. People Will Increase Outcomes

3. People Will End The Relationship

1. People Will Reduce Inputs

Think about a relationship in which you experienced the frustration of Under-Reward. Did you try and even the score by giving less to the relationship? Probably. In organizations, Under-Rewarded people will most certainly find ways to even the score. How? They will:

- Come to work later
- Do less work

- Do careless work
- Call in sick
- Taking extended breaks and lunch hours
- "Forget" to carry out instructions

And, as we all know, there have been several tragic cases where people have felt so Under-Rewarded that they have resorted to violence against their bosses and coworkers.

People have very little trouble figuring out how to restore equity in work relationships. An executive once told us about his resentment at being passed over for an important promotion. He decided to find another job. But while he was looking for that job, he simply sat around his office, doing as little as possible. He says that he felt a certain sense of satisfaction when he finally resigned three months later, because in some small way he had evened the score.

Another person described his high school summer job working in a peach packing shed. His job was to top off each basket with the best looking peaches from off a conveyor belt. Doing so would mean that peach buyers who opened the baskets to inspect them think that each basket contained only the finest peaches.

One night, when he and two coworkers were angered by having to work until midnight four shifts in a row, the three of them began topping off randomly chosen baskets with small, bruised, and even rotten peaches. Although he feels guilty today about engaging in this act of sabotage, at the time, he and his coworkers felt enormous satisfaction at the owner's embarrassment when buyers claimed that the company was trying to sell bad peaches.

Even professional baseball players sometimes reduce their Inputs to restore equity. Some years ago a study of players in their free agency year (the final year of their contract) discovered that many players were having down years in which batting averages, runs batted in, and other measures of a player's effectiveness dropped. You'd think that they would try harder during their free agency year so as to have more leverage when bargaining with a new team. But the researchers who conducted the study concluded that a subconscious desire to get a payback for low salaries in the past was much stronger than a conscious wish to have a good year to improve their bargaining position for the future.

2. People Will Increase Outcomes

People who feel Under-Rewarded can also try to even their Equity Score by trying to change their Outcomes from a relationship. At work, people will ask for:

- Pay raises
- Promotions
- Increased job security
- Job transfers
- Better working conditions

If they don't get what they ask for, employees might increase their Outcomes in other, more destructive ways:

- Working on personal projects while at work
- Padding expense accounts
- Taking company property home
- Stealing from the company
- Sabotage their own work and other people's, too

Maybe these actions don't really even the score, but, even so, they do let employees feel they're doing something to restore equilibrium to the relationship.

Stealing, unfortunately, is one of the ways in which employees try to restore equity, and it's a lot more widespread than most people think. Studies have found that nearly two-thirds of all fast-food restaurant robberies involve current or former employees! In addition, a 1999 National Food Service Security Council found that about half of all restaurant workers have admitted to stealing some form of cash, property or both – and those statistics do not include stealing food.

Stealing to restore equity happens farther up the corporate ladder as well. An executive recently told us how outraged she was when she discovered that one of her subordinates was being paid $2,300 more than she was. She immediately confronted her plant manager. He confirmed that she was indeed making less money than her subordinate.

"I wish I could do something about it, but the company simply has to pay more to get good people these days," he told her.

Several weeks later, she quit her job. As she was emptying her desk, she slipped a dictionary that belonged to her employer into her briefcase.

"I've never stolen anything in my life," she told us. "But for some reason I just picked it up and carried it out." As she passed through security, she was terrified that someone might want to check what was in her briefcase. No one did. And today that book gathers dust on a shelf in her study. She calls it "my $2,300 dictionary."

3. People Will End the Relationship

The third way that Under-Rewarded people restore equity is simply to end the relationship. As we told you earlier, each day across this country thousands of people quit their jobs.

Obviously, quitting a job doesn't bring equity back to the relationship. But for some frustrated people, there appears to be no better option. The stress of being shortchanged in a very important relationship in their life finally drives them to break the relationship off completely. Usually, they've tried other means first to restore the balance, and those efforts have failed. They decided to leave before the inequity gets even

Categories of Equity Sensitivity

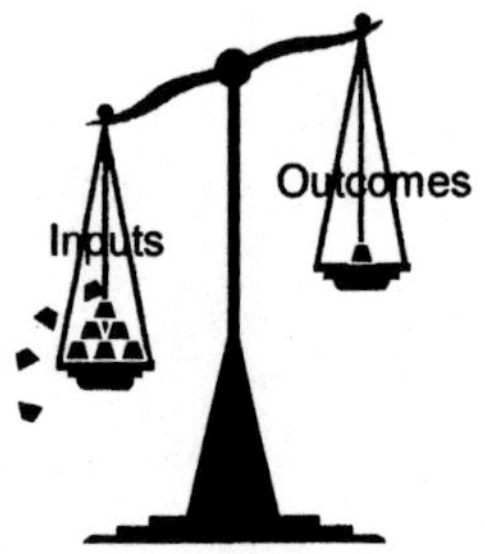

Benevolents
Prefer to give rather than get

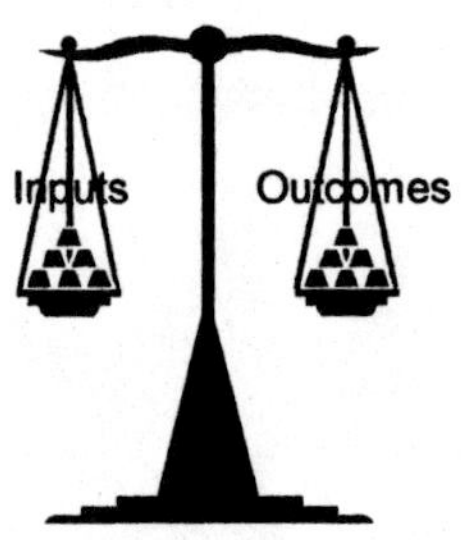

Equity Sensitives
Prefer a balance between what they give and get

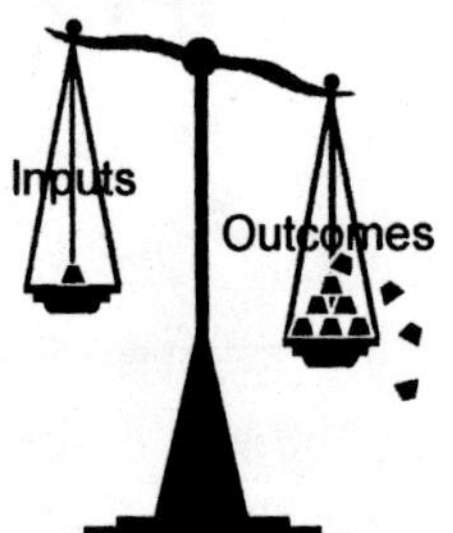

Entitleds
Prefer to get rather than give

worse. And, in today's job market, choosing to quit might actually improve someone's situation considerably.

What the three Laws of Equity tell us is that people want equity in their relationships at work with their bosses, subordinates, coworkers, and organizations – just as they want the same kind of fairness at home with their significant others, children and friends. When they feel that the relationship is out of balance, they'll do everything in their power to restore that give-to-get equilibrium, even if they've got to end the relationship to do it.

Personal Reactions to Equity

Maybe you're troubled by the concept of people always expecting something in return for their contributions to a relationship. You might be saying to yourself, "That's not me. I give a lot, and I don't expect much in return."

During the past several years, we've discovered exceptions to the Equity Laws. In fact, we developed a little analytical tool we call the Equity Sensitivity Test. Having given this test to thousands of people, we can honestly say that some people, in fact, actually do want to give more than they get. We call these people **Benevolents**. Many others, though, prefer to get more than they give. We call them **Entitleds**. But most people do look for a balance between their Inputs and Outcomes – between what they give and what they get. We call people in this category **Equity Sensitives**.

Benevolents

This group is by far the smallest. They usually follow the old Calvinistic philosophy that it is "better to give than receive." They prefer that they give more than they get for several reasons. Some are altruistic people who simply want to do for others, no matter what the return might be. Still others give more than they get so they can feel good about themselves. Benevolents are the givers in relationships.

Entitleds

Entitleds are the getters in relationships. Some Entitleds are members of the "Me" generation – people who would get ahead without doing rather than get ahead by doing. Yet, many Entitleds are extremely talented and valuable players in the workplace. In some instances, it is not surprising that employees are taking more of an entitlement perspective in regard to their jobs. As a result of the loss of the old workplace contract, they see many corporations taking the position that "It's all about shareholder value... everything else is secondary." Is it any wonder that some employees have adopted a similar motto, "I have to take care of me first, and the company comes second?"

Equity Sensitives

Most of us, though, are Equity Sensitives. We try to keep a balance between what we give and what we get from our relationships. We take the temperature of our work relationships by constantly gauging what we contribute to them and what we get in return.

In short, Equity is the most powerful motivation behind why people behave, perform and react the way that they do in work relationships. The Equity Equation explains why people are unproductive, unsatisfied, uncommitted and unhappy at work. Managing equity, though, involves the ability to understand, recognize and consider people's perceptions of what they give and what they get.

In the next chapter, you'll see how people come to look at Inputs and Outcomes the way they do.

Chapter 5
Perceptions of Equity

Harry had worked for his company for nearly 24 years. During those years, he had devoted long days and many weekends to his job. He'd been out of town much of the time and missed more family vacations than he'd been able to take. According to his wife, Harry was "married" to his job. That was exactly the way she put it when she asked for a separation two years ago. They had reconciled, but Harry's marriage hadn't really improved measurably.

Despite difficulties in his personal life, Harry was now within days of achieving his most significant professional goal: promotion to national sales manager. A senior vice president had told Harry confidentially that he was the leading contender for the position and that the company's president would make the announcement the following Monday.

"At last," Harry thought. "All the weekends away from the family, all the nights at the office, all the time, energy and, yes, even love, that I've given this company is going to pay off. I deserve that job, and I think the company knows it."

Then Monday came and went, and so did Harry's shot at the job. The president announced that it was going to someone ten years younger. Bitter, angry and disappointed, Harry made an appointment with the president to find out why he'd been passed over.

"I've devoted my life to this company. My region has been tops in sales the last four years. I deserve this job," he thought. In fact, that's exactly what he told the president.

The president was polite, but firm. "The job's too big for you," he said, evenly.

Harry began to protest, but the president cut him off. "Harry, you know you've got a tough time just handling your own region. From what I hear, you're working nights and weekends all the time. When's the last time you took a vacation with your family? No, this job's way too much for you to handle."

Harry walked slowly from the president's office, his shoulders slouched, his spirit crushed. The words leaped into his mind, "After all I've done for them..." Meanwhile, the company president leaned back in his chair, musing, "Someday he'll thank me for saving him from himself."

Clearly, the two views of what's been given and what's been received are poles apart. Harry sees himself as having devoted much of his life to the company, but that when it came time for the company to reward him, he got nothing. All that he's given to the company has been, he believes, forgotten, ignored or unappreciated. The president, on the other hand, sees his contribution to the relationship as having saved a valued employee from destroying himself professionally. And, somewhere in between, are the facts as they really exist, unseen and not understood by either of them.

This situation between Harry and his boss is a glimpse into a truism of corporate life – that this world doesn't consist of facts and reality, but of ***perceptions*** of facts and reality. These differences play a highly important role in human relationships, especially when it comes to equity and how we perceive equity in the workplace. In every relationship, there are three faces of equity:

- How we see it
- How the other person sees it
- And, somewhere in between, reality

Remember that 53% of managers and 83% of hourly employees in a number of large corporations said they are Under-Rewarded at work. Are they really? The facts might say yes; they might say no. What's important is that if employees perceive themselves as getting the rotten end of the deal, they will act accordingly. Many business leaders have been surprised and baffled at learning how their employees truly feel, leaving the leaders and the employees both saying, "After all I've done for you..."

It's hard to believe that such a huge percentage of people in organizations truly are being shortchanged. In fact, they probably aren't, at least by objective measures. But these people do feel that they are, and that means they are resentful. They will try to find ways, productive and/or destructive, to restore what they see as the balance between what they're giving and what they're getting.

The big question here is, how can people so easily misunderstand or misinterpret the actual facts? How can so many people possibly believe they're being treated so unfairly?

The answer is, that's how they perceive it. It's essential for any leader to understand how people perceive things. If you understand how perception works, you'll have a much better understanding of how employees come up with the sometimes surprising conclusions they do.

The World of Perception

Some time ago, we were sitting in an airport between flights. Near us, employees who had gathered into a small knot were talking heatedly with each other about their relationship with management and their strike, which had ended recently. One of the employees launched a series of blistering comments about management by saying, "Yeah, and the last time they *threw* us out on strike..."

We suspect that the airline's management didn't ever "throw" anybody out on strike, but the employee's comment illustrates just how people can recall matters in very surprising ways.

The writer, Aldous Huxley, once stated that people are capable of accurately recalling everything that has ever happened to them and perceiving everything that is now happening in the universe. Obviously, recalling and perceiving everything would be overwhelming. The mind would have so much information to process at one time that making sense out of any of it would be impossible.

Fortunately, nature has equipped all of us with certain physical limitations that act as filters, helping us sort through what is happening around us. Fortunately, and sometimes unfortunately, we also have developed certain psychological limitations. These limitations sometimes help us and sometimes hinder us in our attempts to see the world as it truly is. Here's how both of these kinds of limitations work.

Physical Limitations

People perceive the world in one of five ways – sight, hearing, taste, touch, and smell. If your senses aren't impaired, they operate twenty-four hours a day. Consider what science tells you about these senses.

Light is a form of electromagnetic wave. Light waves travel through space at 186,000 miles per second. And you see light. Radar, radio signals, and x-rays are also electromagnetic waves. They also travel at 186,000 miles per second. But you don't see them. Although you might want to see radar signals transmitted from police cars, physical limitations do not allow you to do so. So you buy a radar detector, mount it on the dashboard of your car, and let it "see" for you.

The simple fact is that light waves account for less than 2% of all those electromagnetic waves rushing past you at this moment. Imagine how muddled your mind would be if you could see the electromagnetic waves emerging from radio stations in your community or the radar waves emitted from planes flying overhead.

Sound also travels in wave patterns. These wave patterns vibrate, and you hear them. "Normal" hearing means that you can hear sound waves that vibrate between 15 and 15,000 times a second. In older people who are experiencing some hearing loss, the upper limit drops to around 4,000. Among young children, the upper limit can be as high as 30,000. Thus, they hear better than you do as an adult, although any parent will likely testify that his of her child is an exception!

If you could hear sound waves that vibrate fewer than 15 times per second, then, like a robin, you could hear earthworms moving beneath the ground. But you'd also hear your muscles expand and contract as you move your arms and legs. And you'd be plagued by the sound of your blood rumbling through your veins and arteries.

If there were bats in your neighborhood (or in your attic), then you'd be absolutely miserable if you could hear better than the average human being. Bats find their way in the dark by sending out sound waves that vibrate between 50,000 and 90,000 times a second. These sound waves bounce off objects (cave walls, tiny insects, your house) and back to the bats' – and now your – ears.

If your ears were really sensitive, hearing yourself chewing would be like hearing a series of explosions every time your teeth came together. That's an experience you're probably glad to miss.

Physical limitations affect your other senses as well. For example, most birds have a wonderfully keen sense of hearing but almost no sense of smell. Yet the human sense of smell is finely developed, and often the only difference between French cuisine and an ordinary meal is the impact that food has on the olfactory receptors inside your nose. This is because you can taste only bitter, sweet, salty, and sour. Actually, when we eat, all five senses come together. Maybe that's why mealtime is such a big hit with many of us.

So, nature's physical limitations help us perceive better because we don't need to perceive everything. Although you might sometimes want to remove these limitations, they normally protect you from being overloaded with sensory information.

Psychological Limitations

Psychological limitations are very closely tied to how people see equity in their relationships. The limitations here are products of your individual personal history. They could be shaped by your upbringing, your heredity, where you've lived, where you went to school, a book you read, a friend you've known, and a whole slew of other factors as well. Like fingerprints, psychological limitations are unique to every person, even people you're related to. Your limitations are not the same as your mother, father, brother, sister, aunt or uncle. How you yourself perceive the world will dramatically affect your individual perceptions of reality.

For example, nearly everyone today has either a pager or cell phone with them wherever they go. These devices have the ability to be programmed by their owner to have a special ring or activation mechanism. In essence, they allow us to program a psychological limitation into both the equipment and ourselves so that when – and only when – we hear our "special" ring, we will react.

You already know that physical limitations keep the physical world from overloading you. Well, you yourself also operate to keep from being overloaded psychologically. Just as with the way you program your cell phone or pager, you learn to attend to some things and not attend to others.

How do you decide what's important enough to pay attention to? Right at the top of the list are those matters that relate to what you want out of life, your personal goals and objectives. That's why people who have cell phones pay attention to cell phone commercials, people who have dentures pay attention to denture commercials, and dog owners are less likely to hit the TV remote control's mute button if a dog food advertisement flashes on the screen.

Paying such close attention to what matters to you is why you and most everyone else pay close attention to what relates to their personal Equity Equation. People have learned that a primary goal in life is maintaining a balance between what they give and what they get. So at work, people attend carefully to everything that might affect their Inputs and Outcomes on the job. Such issues might include pay raises, overtime, possible mergers or buyouts, who is being promoted or demoted, memos describing benefits reductions or increases, new work hours policies, and rumors about layoffs.

People attend to equity. But the cause of many problems is how they interpret what they pay attention to. That's why the "facts" would probably not confirm that 53% of managers and 83% of employees are actually Under-Rewarded at work – they only feel they are.

It is interesting how even simple words and phrases can bring about different reactions, depending on the psychological limitations you have developed. In the world of perception, the same exact word can mean entirely different things to different people. Equity is not a matter of facts or reality. Instead, it is a matter of fragile, peculiar, and sometimes slanted perceptions of reality. Too often we are disappointed when others do not seem to appreciate or understand what we've done for them.

For example, consider the following chart which lists some terms understood quite differently by top management when compared to mid- and lower- level employees.

Perceptual Differences Between
Top Management and Mid/Lower Level Employees

Term	Meaning for Top Management	Meaning for Mid/Lower Levels
Recession	Perhaps no performance bonus	Perhaps no job
Overtime	Unacceptable payroll expense	Welcomed extra cash
Merger	Increase in shareholder value and my stock options	Major transition & threat to job security

Turkeys, Skunks, and Sharks

If you've ever visited a turkey farm, then you know turkeys are not very smart. During thunderstorms, some turkeys literally don't have sense enough to come in out of the rain. Instead, they tilt their heads back, open their beaks and drink until they drown. The turkeys in the turkey house all rush to a corner for protection. Problem is, they all tend to rush to the same corner, sometimes resulting in a feathered pile of crushed and smothered turkeys.

Even though they're not very smart, female turkeys tend to be good mothers, but only if something very specific triggers that reaction. They diligently watch and protect their young, spending much of their time warming their chicks beneath their wings. This behavior apparently is triggered by a distinctive, high-pitched "cheep, cheep" sound young turkeys make. It's that precise sound which makes the difference. A young turkey's smell, appearance or touch plays almost no role in eliciting a mother's protective behavior. In fact, if a baby turkey for some reason doesn't make that "cheep, cheep" sound, the mother will abandon or, in some cases, kill the chick.

The mother turkey's almost total reliance on that single sound for identifying her young can and does produce some strange behavior. The animal behaviorist, M.S. Fox, did an experiment with mother turkeys and a stuffed skunk. Skunks are a natural enemy of turkeys. Generally, whenever a skunk approaches, a mother turkey will flap her wings, squawk, peck and claw at the skunk to drive it away. Fox's experiment showed that the mother turkeys would react that way even toward a stuffed skunk, pulled by a string toward a mother turkey – until the tape recorder inside the stuffed skunk made a "cheep, cheep" sound.

Then, the mother turkey would stop her violent attacks and even occasionally try to draw the skunk under her wing. But as soon as the tape recorder was turned off and the "cheep, cheep" stopped, the mother turkey would attack once again.

This experiment shows that we should all be grateful that, as a human being, we are able to think, understand, and perceive the world around us better than any mother turkey.

But just because we have better perception skills than a turkey doesn't mean we always get things right. Consider the answers to the following four questions:

Question 1: **How many people in the United States die each year of skin cancer?** 9,600 – yet most of us continue to sunbathe.

Question 2: **How many people in the United States die each year in auto accidents?** Nearly 43,500 – yet 86% of the population 15 years and older have driver's licenses.

Question 3: **How many people in the United States dies each year of diseases related to smoking?** More than 430,000 – yet approximately 53 million Americans continue to smoke (with 3,000 young people becoming daily smokers every day).

Question 4: **How many swimmers die each year from shark attacks WORLDWIDE? –** Ten people in 2000 (only one of which was in the U.S.). The average for the decade is 7 per year worldwide.

Armed with these statistics, the next time you are near the ocean, walk down to the beach and gingerly step over all the people lying there soaking up the sun's rays and scorching their skin. Wade into the surf until it gets about knee-high. Then, at the top of your lungs, yell two words. No, it's not "cheep cheep." It's "Shark! Shark!" Then stand back and watch the "turkeys…"

- Scramble out of the water
- Stumble over the sunbathers
- Jump into their cars
- Light up a cigarette
- Then drive to safety

OK, you know you won't actually try this little experiment, but you get the point. People are susceptible to what we call "Shark Syndrome Perception." Despite having a finely tuned capacity for understanding the world around them, people often perceive only what they want to in their relationships and their surroundings, no matter what the facts are and despite the efforts of reasonable people to convince them otherwise. Sharks are considered to be big, mean and ugly (thanks in large part to the advent of the JAWS movie series back in 1975), so we perceive them to be by far a greater threat to human life than cigarettes, driving a car and skin cancer – even though the facts prove quite the opposite.

It's the same with you and your employees. Many leaders think that what makes employees whistle while they work is getting fatter paychecks, bigger bonuses and a never-ending list of perks. By now, you should understand that the facts say otherwise. Is pay important? Sure. People who say to themselves, "I don't get PAID enough to do this" are feeling cheated.

But you also should understand that people who work for you or anyone else are never going to give you – their manager/leader – the extra effort, loyalty, the imagination and creativity they possess, unless they believe you deserve it and want to give it to you voluntarily. So...

- If you accept that your employees are in a relationship with you and your company that is based on the Equity Equation (i.e., you realize that they give to you and the company so they will get something back)...

- If you accept that many of your employees may feel they're giving more than they're getting from you and the organization; that continued downsizings, mergers, acquisitions and other strategies which are focused on pumping up the company's stock price are a very important reason employees are feeling shortchanged in their Equity Equation at work...

- And, if you realize that those of your employees who feel Under-Rewarded may be inclined to rebalance the Equity Equation by withholding the creativity, focus, performance and extra effort you need from them...

...then you are ready to discover how to begin paying out **The Hidden Paycheck**.

Putting The Hidden Paycheck Into Practice

The Hidden Paycheck can be effectively and equitably paid on two levels:

- The Hidden Paycheck can be distributed on an organizational level, and;

- The Hidden Paycheck can be paid out on a day-to-day basis through the immediate manager, whether it's the CEO, executive, mid-level manager or front-line supervisor.

On an organizational level, corporations can pay attention to how the company's practice and policies fit into the Equity Equation. Many CEOs and top leaders may not think of such policies in terms of the give-to-get relationship they have with their employees – but their employees certainly do. Just ask them. Almost any employee can tell you how their organization's policies reflect how much he or she is getting for what they're giving.

Organizations can put into place practices that will help rebalance the Equity Equation all over the company. Each of these practices is geared toward providing employees with the feeling that they're getting from the company as good as they're giving to it. You can read more about these High Payoff Practices in Appendix A.

However, we realize that many of you may not be in a position where you can effectively control or influence what the practices your company engages in. There may be little you can do about whether your organization, as a whole, decides to pay the Hidden Paycheck to all employees.

But, *you* can offer it to *your* employees. This book is largely written for you and how as an individual manager/leader, you can provide the Hidden Paycheck to the people who work directly for you. While providing equity on an organizational level is important, your role is actually more crucial to rebalancing the Equity Equation for your employees. In fact, you are *the single most important influence* in providing your employees equity on a day-to-day basis.

Why should you want to start paying your people the Hidden Paycheck? If your team is more efficient, packs higher productivity into every hour, and produces the kind of performance you've only imagined up to now, then your company becomes more profitable. And that fact reflects directly on you and your leadership abilities.

Just turn the page, and Part II will show you how to get a lot of mileage out of paying the Hidden Paycheck.

Part II:

PAYING THE HIDDEN PAYCHECK: YOUR ROLE AS THE IMMEDIATE MANAGER/LEADER

You do not lead by hitting people over the head –

That's assault, not leadership.

– Dwight D. Eisenhower

Chapter 6
The Key to Unlocking the Hidden Paycheck: The Immediate Manager/Leader

Years ago, while we were doing some work for IBM, we began to grasp just how crucial the immediate manager is to how employees view the entire organization. After conducting an annual employee opinion survey, top IBM management decided it would look at two groups: the top 10 locations where employees had the highest job satisfaction and were most committed to the company, and the bottom 10 locations which ranked lowest on both these scales.

When they compared the survey responses for the top and bottom locations, management found that employees at the top locations had much more favorable perceptions of pay and benefits than employees at the bottom locations, who generally thought they were underpaid and benefits were not very good. As you might suspect with a company like IBM, when actual salaries and benefits received by employees at both the top and bottom locations were compared, the pay structures were essentially the same – there was virtually no difference in the actual salaries and benefits for those two groups of employees.

Intrigued by this finding, IBM management then examined how employees responded to the other survey questions (nearly 150 survey items in all). They discovered only one question that showed a major

The IBM Story:
The Impact of Two Way Communication

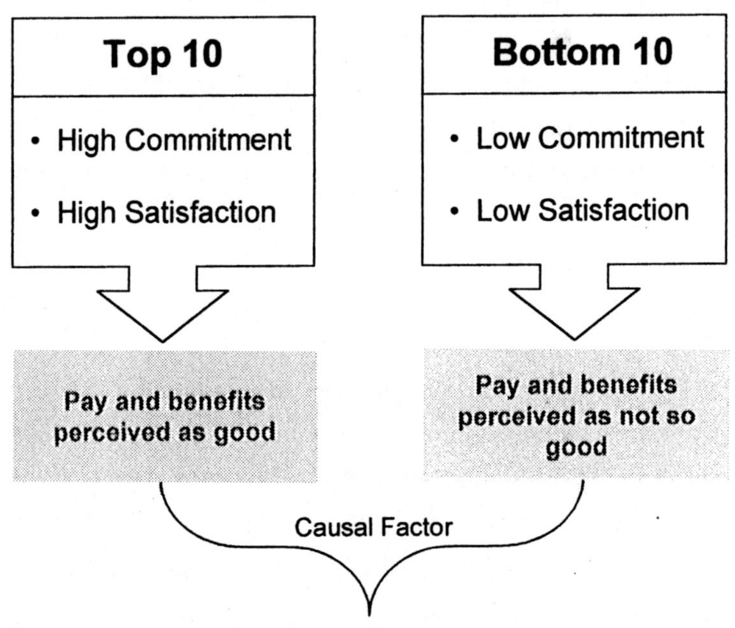

Two-way communication with my immediate manager

difference between the top and bottom locations – **two-way communication with my immediate manager**.

Those employees who worked at the top locations (again, in terms of job satisfaction and commitment to IBM) felt that two-way communication with their immediate managers was very good. Employees at the bottom locations thought they had very little communication with their immediate managers. Somehow, managers who engaged in two-way communication with their employees were having a dramatic impact on how their employees looked at pay and benefits, even though communication and pay seemed entirely unrelated to each other.

Shortly after we completed our findings at IBM, we came across some studies from the U.S., the United Kingdom and Australia. These studies asked employees whom they preferred to be their primary source of information within their organizations. The overwhelming response: their immediate manager, especially in times of turbulence or transition.

This finding goes up against traditional approaches to communication: that it should come from the top. Whether it's from the CEO or head office, this kind of communication is not very effective.

A top executive giving a speech at a podium, or distributing company newsletters and bulletins, or creating posters and slogans, are all very popular

Preferred Source of Information for Employees

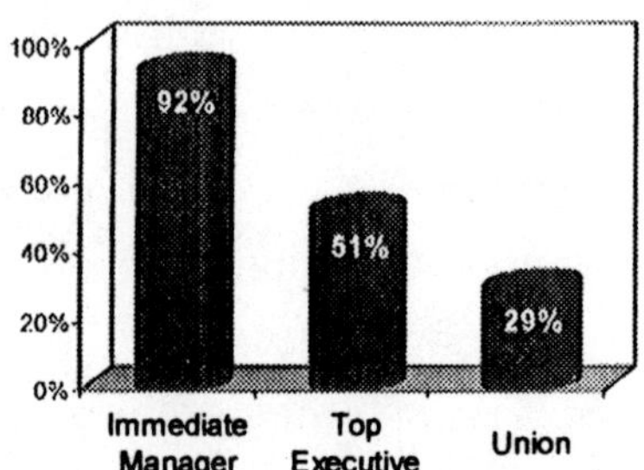

United States

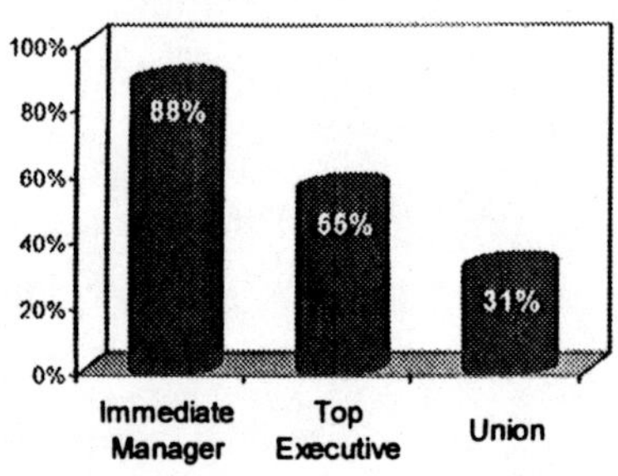

United Kingdom

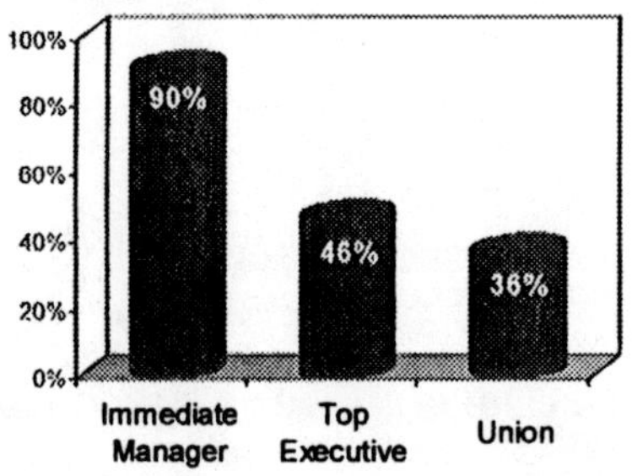

Canada

ways to communicate within an organization. The assumption is that employees will take a message more to heart if it comes from the organization's highest authorities, which are supposedly the sources employees believe the most readily. Wrong. Dead wrong. Just ask the employees. When they're asked where they want their information about the company to come from, they choose their immediate manager almost every time.

General Motors knows this fact to be true. After GM management heard about the other studies, they decided to conduct one of their own to see if their employees felt the same way. They did.

Preferred Source of Information at GM

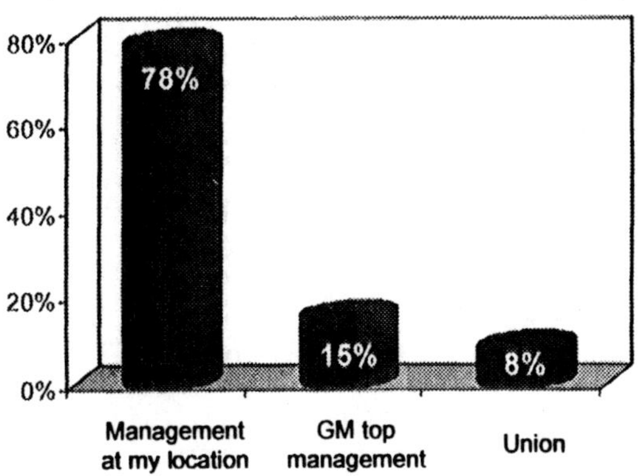

Again, the immediate manager was the overwhelming choice. Employees would much rather receive information from their immediate managers than they would from the corporate office.

While we tend to celebrate great companies…

In reality, there are only great managers.

– Marcus Buckingham
Senior Consultant
The Gallup Organization

The Immediate Manager/Leader and Performance

In 1999, the Gallup organization published findings from a multi-year study it had conducted that took the previous findings about the importance of the immediate manager to new levels. They analyzed what impact, if any, the manager/employee relationship had on several critical business outcomes including customer loyalty and profitability. Gallup based their results on interviews with over 100,000 employees from over 2,500 work units in 12 different industries.

Their key findings were as follows:

- Work groups with positive employee attitudes are **50%** more likely to deliver on customer loyalty.

- Work units in the top quartile in terms of positive employee attitudes accounted for a **24% higher profit** than work units in the bottom quartile.

- **And... the immediate manager at every level has the greatest impact on employee attitude and satisfaction.**

So, if positive employee attitudes and job satisfaction boost customer loyalty and profits – and the immediate manager is the most powerful factor in shaping employee attitude and satisfaction (i.e., their perceptions of Equity Equation) – it follows then that the immediate manager, not the CEO, not the people with the big titles and the corner offices (except with their own direct reports),. is the person with the biggest clout in determining how well the company does. Think about that. By bringing the Equity Equation into balance with your employees, you help them perceive they're getting as much as they're giving. Their attitude gets better, their job satisfaction climbs higher, and their performance takes a leap forward, profits go up – and your own personal star shines more brightly.

In fact, we will take this concept and "kick it up a notch." Our contention is that the immediate manager/leader at every level is not only ***a*** driver of performance and profit – but is ***the*** driver of performance and profit within organizations. That's why the rest of this chapter will detail why sharpening a strong and enduring positive relationship between the immediate manager/leaders and the people who report to them is the most cutting-edge competitive advantage organizations can leverage today.

Yes, that's you. Just by making sure your employees feel they're getting as much as they're giving, you can spark performance and profit far better than anyone else. Many leaders try to get better results by pushing employees again and again to get them to go faster and faster. You can't drive your employees that way for very long before they drop in a heap of exhaustion and resentment. For good performance over the long haul, show your people you appreciate them and they'll jump over the moon for you.

The Fallacy Within The Current Leadership Model

If you accept that the immediate manager/leader at every level is the person who gives the biggest boost (or the biggest boot) to how well employees within an organization perform, then you're in direct violation of the leadership model so lovingly embraced by most of Corporate America today.

Most companies, especially the big ones, currently worship at the leadership altar of the CEO. After World War II, many companies began mimicking the military's "Where the general leads, we will follow" approach to leadership... an approach that is still quite popular in the new millennium.

The corporate propensity to place all eggs in executive baskets has led to a pay gap the size of the Grand Canyon between top leadership and other people at lower levels of the organization. Looking at executive salaries for the last 20 years, a recent *Executive Pay Watch* report showed that:

- In 1980, the average CEO of a major corporation earned 42 times more than the typical American blue-collar worker.
- In 1990, the difference was 85 times the average factory wage.
- In 1999, this pay disparity had skyrocketed to 475 times the average factory wage.

The current leadership model which overemphasizes the CEO and a select few at the top is not in alignment with what we now know to be the true driver of performance and profit…

…the immediate manager at every level of the organization.

– Richard C. Huseman, Ph.D.

Some defenders of the current executive compensation model would point out that companies are forced to offer extremely generous compensation packages in order to secure the best talent they can. In their minds, the individual they select as their CEO will be the determining factor between the future success or ruin of the company. And, the executive who accepts the challenge to lead the company should be well compensated for the risks they must be willing to take – both personally and professionally.

Whoa! Think about this for a moment. What risk is the CEO assuming? Is it the risk that they won't get paid well if they don't produce amazing results? They seem to get buckets of money no matter whether their performance is spectacular or rotten. There are numerous instances of companies who turned in less-than-stellar profits and still pay their CEOs exorbitant salaries for producing only mediocre results.

Poster Children in Executive Excess:
A Five-Year Performance Comparison

Company	CEO	Cumulative 5-Year Total Pay	Stock Performance vs. S&P 500
Sprint	William Esrey	$218.4 mill.	↓ 34%
Conseco	Stephen Hilbert	$146.2 mill.	↓ 50%

Note: We are not condemning the entrepreneurial CEO who took the risk to start and build a new company from scratch. Many of those entrepreneurs struggled for years before they got the big payback. Rather, we are questioning CEOs who are brought in to fill the top spot who have risked nothing to start the company and who face no real financial risk if they don't perform well.

Even when times are bad, it doesn't seem like these CEOs are paying the price.

With this in mind, some companies have adapted an approach that would link CEO compensation with company performance. The way they do this is by offering stock options as a part of the compensation packages for top executives. The thinking goes something like this; if a portion of an executive's pay is directly tied to how well the company's stock is doing, then that executive is going to make sure that their leadership is in line with making that stock price as strong as possible. Top management and shareholder interests would be aligned.

This actually makes some sense. If a company is doing well, their executives share in the profits. If a company isn't doing well, then executives pay the price, too. Right?

Wrong. When bad times do come, many companies back away from their original agreements and offer their top executives a nice, comfy cushion to soften the impact to their stock options. The popular term for this is "option repricing." Companies who engage in option repricing basically take the original price established for the stock options and reduce these prices to bring them about equal to current stock value. In other words, if executives received their options at $50 dollars and the value of the stock has fallen to below $25 dollars, their companies reprice their options to, let's say, $30 dollars, so that their executives don't actually risk anything near as much as outside shareholders do. Option repricings are quite simply a gift to CEOs and top management that outside shareholders do not receive.

Companies that reprice their stock options argue that these tactics are necessary to keep their coveted CEOs and executives from leaving for sweeter deals someplace else. This, of course, assumes that the departure of these executives would greatly damage the company. But, in a recent academic study, it was reported that there is no evidence that the repricing of options actually improves the financial performance of the company. More over, the study found that companies that use option repricing actually have higher rates of CEO turnover.

The study examined repricings at 100 companies and compared them with similar companies who did not reprice. Interestingly, they found that the first year after a repricing, CEO turnover was 16.3 percent, compared to the 4.7 percent at companies who did not reprice. At the two-year mark, CEO turnover rate at companies that had repriced was 25.5 percent versus the 10.5 percent at companies who did not reprice!

So, ironically, option repricing as a strategy to keep CEOs and other top executives from leaving doesn't seem to be effective and, in some strange way, may actually prompt the departure of these executives from the company.

But, the story of CEO compensation doesn't end here. The last chapter of our analysis of the CEO compensation versus performance relationship is what happens to CEOs when they are fired for poor performance. In many of these cases, CEOs who have been fired don't face any real financial risk due to their poor performance. Consider the following list of CEOs and the exit packages they received after being fired from their companies.

Ousted CEOs In 2000 – The Leader Board

WHO	OUSTED FROM	SEVERANCE*
Douglas Ivester	Coca-Cola	$166 million
Jill Barad	Mattel	$47 million
Dale Morrison	Campbell Soup	$4 million
Richard Thomas	Xerox	$11 million
Durk Jager	Proctor & Gamble	$15 million

**Includes estimated value of pension and stock compensation*

Why are these top leaders getting such big rewards for their poor leadership? It seems that even when they are fired, the equity in their work relationship seems quite high.

So, while the current leadership model has companies protecting their CEOs and other top executives from the financial risks associated with their positions in the hierarchy by:

- Providing exorbitant compensation even when corporate performance is lagging;
- Repricing stock options so even when the company is losing money, executives aren't;
- And, offering big payoffs even when executives are being fired;

...who really is taking the biggest risk within these companies? In our view, it's rank-and-file employees who are taking the biggest risk.

Yet, it is the rank-and-file employees who are charged with the day-to-day implementation of the strategies formulated by the people at the top. If the strategies don't work, it's the rank-and-file employee, even the good performers, who most often gets booted in order to keep the stock price from careening off a cliff – and with nothing even close to the golden parachutes CEOs get for their bad performance.

This gross inequity between how top leadership is paid compared to all the others in an organization wouldn't matter so much if this leadership served up a bigger slice of the economic pie to everyone involved, including the rank and file. But that's not happening. Despite overall productivity increases of more than 30% since 1973, real wages are down by 9%. After adjusting for inflation, rank-and-file workers today earn less than their counterparts did 25 years ago.

Do you think workers don't notice the huge gap between what top executives get paid and what's in their paychecks? Wrong. Recently, we were at an airport (yes, another airport) and started chatting with some of the employees from a commuter airline. They were on strike and picketing vigorously. Those employees told us that if their CEO gave up $9 million from his salary – which still would have left him with $3 million-plus a year – each employee would get an additional $7,000. Whether these figures are accurate or not, we don't know. What is important is that regardless of the truth, this is what these employees believe.

Considering that the current starting annual salary for pilots with this airline is in the $20,000 range, and the copilots start in the $16,000 range, that $7,000 a year could mean the difference between buying a car – or not – buying a house – or not – and sending their children to college – or not.

In short, the current leadership model has several flaws. First, it devotes the majority of its attention, resources and hopes for the future on a select group of individuals and many companies are not getting the return on their investment that they should be.

Second, the top-down approach to running a company and the huge pay gaps it generates between top executives and others in the organization makes the already tipped Equity Scale even more one-sided. Employees see these pay gaps and believe they're getting a whole lot less than they're giving. The result: The loyalty and effort organizations get from their employees continues to dwindle.

Finally, the current leadership model is missing the boat in terms of really focusing on how to secure high performance and profit in the long term – no matter how good a CEO you have, there are just some things they can't do – things that you, as the immediate manager/leader, can.

A Contrarian Approach To Leadership

For many people, what we are proposing is heresy. They think that, just because the CEO and other senior executives are at the top of the corporate hill, they will be the leaders who blaze the trail to profits and productivity for the rest of the company. But relying on a few top executives (and paying them high salaries), as we have shown, will not necessarily secure corporate success.

We suggest a different approach... one that emphasizes leadership at every level of the organization. A company-wide approach that would redirect some of that executive compensation into helping teach and train leaders at

There's a piece of us that we all sort of hold in reserve and we only give it when we are truly committed to what we are trying to achieve.

You get 30% of most people's effort in a normal sense, but there's another 70% that is discretionary and is only given if people really want to give it.

Real leadership is somehow trying to tap that extra 70%.

Brian Baker
President,
North America Marketing & Refining
Mobil Corporation
1999

every level of the organization to pay their direct reports their long-overdue Hidden Paycheck.

It is the immediate manager/leader, be it the CEO, mid-level manager, or front-line supervisor, who can best enhance performance and profit with the people who report directly to them. They have access to the greatest competitive advantage available to organizations now and into the future.

Look. The time is past for looking to making hundreds, thousands, even tens of thousands of employees walk the plank as a way of boosting profits. These strategies have been pretty well tapped out.

Even offering employees high salaries hasn't produced the kind of commitment and productivity companies need from their employees to survive. Good pay will keep people doing enough to keep their jobs. It will not inspire them or guarantee their loyalty and commitment. But, distributing the Hidden Paycheck will. To get your employees' best efforts, you can't bribe them with money alone. You have show them appreciation. You have to show them you recognize their value, and you don't think of them as just being interchangeable units, to be installed or disposed of at will.

By inspiring employees, you can tap into their reservoir of **discretionary effort** – the effort employees choose to give over and above just doing enough to get by. And it's up to you, and every manager/leader like you, to tap it.

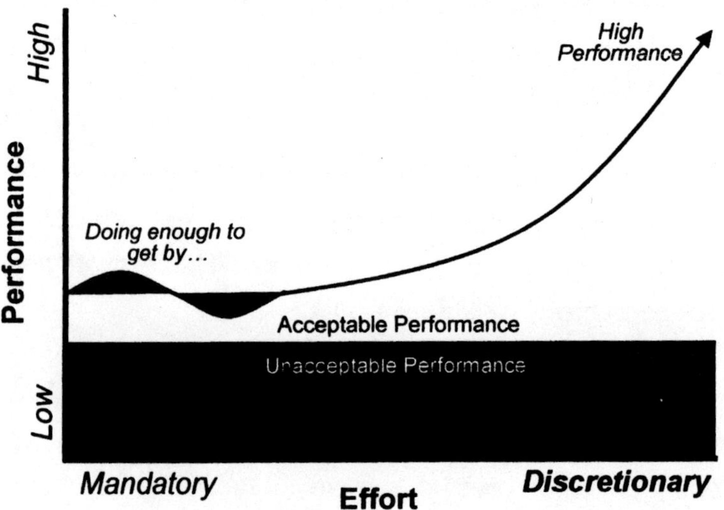
Human Performance
(Mandatory Effort Vs. Discretionary Effort)
High
Performance
Low
High
Performance
Doing enough to
get by...
Acceptable Performance
Unacceptable Performance
Mandatory
Effort
Discretionary

The Concept of Discretionary Effort

If you are an employee and you come into work everyday with the perception that your organization does not value you or what you contribute while on the job, what would you do? Many of us would (and do) respond by working only as hard as we need to so that we don't get fired – we do just enough to get by.

Why would any of us put in any extra effort, energy or initiative at work when we feel that the company might sacrifice us without another thought if the balance sheet needed a boost? When employees have this attitude, then companies get the bare minimum effort of what they need. They don't even come close to getting the effort they want.

Discretionary effort isn't necessarily about working more hours or taking on more responsibilities or jobs. Discretionary effort is what happens when people throw themselves into a job with their head and their heart, voluntarily giving their full attention, focus and creativity toward the attainment of company goals. It's the enthusiasm and drive we've all applied at some time in our life, whether we were playing a favorite sport, working on a pet project or were aiming at winning a prize we very much wanted. At those times, every fiber in our being was focused on achieving our goal – not because we had to, but because we deeply, passionately, wanted to.

For the most part, leaders rarely tap into that drive and passion. If they did, they could inspire superior performance, make their employees happier and more secure, and their customers would be more than satisfied. It is discretionary effort that can guarantee the high performance levels that will beat out the competition and get an organization to meet even its most far-reaching goals.

But again, who is willing to give their discretionary effort in a game where shareholders are positioned as king and employees are viewed as pawns. You have to give to get. How? By understanding how you impact what your employees do (and do not) do.

Understanding The Key To Performance

In the current business environment where the only constant is change, today's success may not be tomorrow's opportunity. The results we need to succeed may change frequently so focusing solely on results may not be nearly as effective as many think it is. There are other factors that impact results – most important of these is ***behavior***. How employees "behave" at work is critical to achieving desired goals while results are merely the final output.

For example, in many organizations, managers zero in on "managing for results," rather than managing behaviors. Let's say a manager wants a 15% sales increase by the end of next quarter. The manager focused solely on results would be fixated on the number of units sold each week. The leader looking to manage behavior, on the other hand, would be assessing and maximizing how employees actually work to improve sales, realizing that results are merely the final output of the many behaviors that came before them. The key issue for leaders and their direct reports is how to focus on the specific key behaviors that will lead to the high performance needed to guarantee success.

The ABC's of Behavior

The **ABC Behavior Model**, long used by behavioral psychologists, is a useful way to understand how you affect performance. This approach says that behavior is driven by two factors: Antecedents and Consequences.

Antecedents

An antecedent is something that occurs prior to a behavior. Within your organization, these antecedents might include instructions, policies, procedures, training, performance goals, vision statements, etc. Antecedents set the stage for a behavior to occur. They do not, however, guarantee that a behavior actually will occur.

Managers use antecedents a lot (setting goals, giving instructions, providing training, etc.). They spend much of their time telling their direct reports what to do, how to do it and under what conditions it must be done. In fact, studies have shown that the majority of managers spend

The ABC Behavior Model

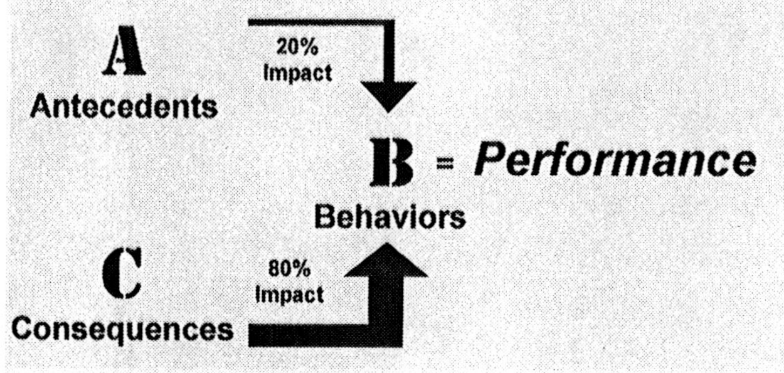

80% of their time with direct reports managing antecedents. But, according to the ABC model, these managers are wasting much of this time if their goal is to really impact the behavior and performance of their employees. It is the application of consequences, not antecedents, which will channel and strengthen the kind of actions you want from your employees. In fact, almost 80% of behavior is actually determined by consequences, not antecedents.

Consequences

If an antecedent is something that happens before a behavior, a consequence, not too surprisingly, is what happens after a behavior occurs or does not occur. A consequence usually is defined in terms of:

- A positive reinforcement, which is a way of inspiring employees to do more of something you want them to do, or

- A negative reinforcement, which is a kind of punishment designed to discourage employees from doing something you don't want them to do.

Positive reinforcements could include a thank you note, or giving a pat on the back for a job well done. Unfortunately, many managers/leaders don't dish out much in terms of positive reinforcement, even during performance reviews. When consequences are used, they are usually negative in nature – a harsh criticism or, in extreme cases, a demotion or reassignment.

The unfortunate truth is that in business today, most managers do not effectively use the ABC Model. They spend most of their time managing antecedents and only focus on consequences during performance reviews or after things have already gone wrong.

Always remember it is the consequence side of the model that has by far the greatest impact on behavior – consequences drive 80% of behavior. Antecedents may jump-start the way people act, but consequences are what keep it going.

For example, consider cigarette smoking. For years, the federal government puzzled over whether cigarette packages should have a warning label on them, then took even longer figuring out what the warning should say. The first message went something like this: "Warning – The Surgeon General has determined that smoking ***MAY BE*** dangerous to your health" (emphasis added).

Not too surprisingly, very few smokers looked at the warning and threw their unlit cigarettes into the trash. So, lawmakers tried again. This time they tried something more hard-hitting: "Warning – the Surgeon General has determined that cigarette smoking ***IS*** dangerous to your health" (emphasis added). Again, the public was not deterred from lighting up, even with the dramatic rewording of the warning (sarcasm added). The antecedent of putting a warning on cigarette packages had virtually no impact on whether people chose to smoke or not.

What has had an effect are other factors (consequences) which are a lot more direct: Hefty fines for people who smoke on planes and public outcry for those who light up in many public restaurants and buildings. The consequences of being hit directly in the pocketbook or the ego if they light up has curtailed far more smokers than any finger-wagging antecedents could have done.

Curtailing cigarette smoking is a lesson in psychology. No matter how enticing or intimidating an antecedent is, it's not going to have a long-lasting effect unless it's paired with a meaningful consequence. If we're in a huge rush, a sign that reads, "Reserved Parking" isn't likely to stop us from parking there, especially if we know we'll only be a minute. But, a sign which reads, "Danger – High Voltage" is much more likely to grab our attention. Why? Because we know that if we ignore the antecedent, the consequences could be literally quite shocking.

Consequences Really Do Determine Behavior

Every day, people leave work either more motivated, or less motivated, to come back the next day. What makes the difference? Whatever happened to them that day. Performance is about what happens every day. Each time we do something, something else happens as a result (i.e., a consequence). There are four categories of consequences: Extinction, Punishment, Negative Reinforcement and Positive Reinforcement.

Extinction: You Don't Get What You Want

For example, perhaps you present a new idea to your boss. Even though you offer it several times, the boss seems either too busy or unwilling to listen to you. After a couple more tries, you throw up your hands and never mention the subject again.

Punishment: You Get Something You Don't Want

Suppose you miss a meeting because you wrote the wrong date into your calendar. As a result, you lose a potential client. From that point forward, you confirm your appointments for the following week on the preceding Friday.

Negative Reinforcement: You Escape or Avoid Something You Don't Want

Even though you know you've got many more important things to do than your monthly expense report, you do it anyway. You know if you don't, your boss, her boss and the accounting department will be all over your back the next day if you don't turn the report in on time.

Positive Reinforcement: You Get Something You Want

Your boss offers to upgrade your computer. She has two reasons, she tells you. One is so getting your job done will be easier. Second, she tells you she wants her best player to be even more effective than you already are.

As a result, your performance shoots up, not just because your equipment is now sportier but also because you just got a major ego boost.

Of these four categories, two (Positive and Negative Reinforcement), help increase performance. Two others (Punishment and Extinction), reduce performance. Many leaders work under the mistaken assumption that if people are performing well that there's no need to say anything. Bad idea. Doing nothing is a consequence. It means that no matter how good a job your team members do, you won't reward them in any way. Soon they'll stop trying and performance will drop. So, not doing anything is actually a form of extinction.

You as a leader change the behavior of your employees both by what you do *and* what you don't do. The consequences you do or do not provide are actually among the most important Outcomes your employees are seeking in their Equity Equation.

Consequences and the Equity Equation

So, think back to the Equity Equation. Your employees through their hard work are providing Inputs into their work relationship. What you do or don't do about their hard work provides their Outcomes. In other words, you have a powerful opportunity to shape what your employees do and how well they do it. So, take a look at what you can do to provide Consequences to your employees. Try the following Consequence Quiz:

1. Are the consequences you provide positive or negative?

2. Do you provide consequences right away or do you allow some time to pass after the behavior occurs to actually give them?

3. Are the consequences certain, or do your employees wonder what (if any) consequences will be given?

If you said that the consequences you give your employees are:

☑ POSITIVE
☑ IMMEDIATE
☑ CERTAIN

then you're using consequences in a way that gets your employees to do what you want them to do. However, if your consequences are:

☑ NEGATIVE
☑ IN THE FUTURE
☑ UNCERTAIN

then you're shooting yourself in the foot. You aren't encouraging your people to act the way you want and, in fact, you may be encouraging them to act in ways you don't want. That means performance levels head south, and guess who looks bad as a result? (For the answer to this riddle, take a long, deep look in the mirror.)

The Role of Consequence History

You may be asking yourself if consequences come after a behavior, how can they possibly have an 80% impact on behavior? It's a bit like who came first, the chicken or the egg. Remember that we're all walking around with that equity calculator in our heads, keeping track of what we give and what we get and checking to see if the two balance out. That calculator is always on full alert to gauge the consequences that result from our behavior.

For example, suppose a minor issue at work has come up, and you decide to bring it to the attention of your boss. You go into her office and share your concern with her. Then she scowls and says, "The company doesn't react well to problems. Top management isn't really interested in your ideas. You need to focus on just doing your job."

You automatically log this conversation into your behavior calculator. Later, when an even bigger issue comes up, you'll look back in your history of consequences and decide that you're going to keep your mouth shut. The earlier consequence of having your boss slap you down for bringing a problem to her attention has transformed into an antecedent that discourages you from speaking up this time around.

Consequences get fed into our behavior calculator in two ways: directly and indirectly. Your boss telling you to mind your own business is an example of the direct path, when consequences become burned into our mind from our own personal experience. Most consequences, though, come to us indirectly. That's when you pick up on what you hear about other people's consequences. You don't have to try leaping out of a plane without a parachute to know that the consequences will be pretty unpleasant. And, many corporate cultures are prime breeding grounds for indirect, negative consequences.

For example, suppose you and a coworker are in a two-hour meeting with one of the company's senior executives. The meeting is very productive. However, close to the end, your coworker and friend raises an issue with a decision made at a recent board meeting. The issue is a valid one, but your friend doesn't bring it up in the most tactful way. The senior executive loses his temper, cuts off your friend with a biting response, and ends the meeting abruptly.

Once the meeting is over, even though it was basically very productive, the one fact that gets communicated in rapid-fire fashion throughout the organization is how the senior executive lost his temper when he was asked a seemingly innocent and valid question. As a result, others throughout the organization decide to think twice before they raise any questions they might have with that particular executive. Why? Because their indirect consequence history *predicts* that the result could be negative one, even though they have not witnessed the consequence first hand.

And don't think it stops there. The problem with associating a negative consequence with a particular behavior is that the association can spread. Let's say the temperamental executive we just described is actually a peer of yours and you hold similar titles in different divisions within the company. After hearing about how the other executive lost his cool during the meeting, your people might actually transfer that negative consequence to their relationship with you. They might decide not to ask questions about senior level decision-making because they think they're going to be yelled at, as well – even though you have never even raised your voice or become angry with anyone. You may have told your employees again and again that they can be open and direct in their communications with you and on several occasions, when they have asked you questions, you have tried to give very positive consequences to that behavior. However, one negative consequence – either acquired directly or indirectly – can cancel out many positive consequences in an individual's personal consequence history logbook.

As a manager/leader, if your employees are more likely to predict that their behaviors will result in a negative consequence rather than a positive one, they'll start to curb their behavior. In addition, their resistance will be very high when you try to get them to focus on any new behaviors for increasing performance or implementing some type of change.

Paying The Hidden Paycheck

Here's what you need to accept in order to pay out the Hidden Paycheck to your employees:

- That you, as the group's leader, whether you're the CEO, mid-level manager or front-line supervisor, are the most powerful force in shaping the performance of the people who report directly to you.

- That you as a leader have the strongest impact on how your employees gauge the balance between what they give to the organization (be it talent, skills, loyalty, etc.), compared to what they get back (pay, benefits, a sense of accomplishment, meaningful work, and being valued, etc.).

- That how you relate to your employees and how they feel about the way you relate to them is almost the entire basis for how they feel about the organization as a whole. Time after time, employees say that a "good" manager is the reason they stay with a company, and a "bad" manager is why they quit.

- That you as the leader are the sculptor, the person who most shapes what your employees do for the company and for you. Remember that the ABC Model of behavior says that if you place 20% of your emphasis on Antecedents and 80% of your time on Consequences, you can have a major impact on the behavior of your employees (and, in turn, their performance) at work.

For all of these reasons, you as the immediate manager/leader are the best person to dispense the Hidden Paycheck to your employees. In doing so, you go a long way in rebalancing the Equity Equation in their work relationship with you and your company.

However, paying out that Hidden Paycheck is not without its challenges. The next chapter will show you some of the obstacles you may face in actually distributing the Hidden Paycheck to your employees and getting the performance and profit you need to succeed.

Chapter 7
The Hidden Paycheck Challenge: Why The Equity Equation Is Tough To Manage

Think back to your first day on the job. Chances are you had very positive expectations. You thought of your future in the very best terms of salary increases, promotion and advancement, job security, and job satisfaction. The frustrations of someone else getting credit for your work or getting the promotion you wanted, the hardship of dealing with difficult people, or the possibility of actually being laid off, well, none of these possibilities were among your expectations that first day.

That's how we begin most relationships of any kind – full of high expectations, brimming with the possibilities this new situation can bring. Unfortunately, there's usually a wide gap between the expectations we had at the beginning of a new job and the letdown, frustration and even bitter disappointment we frequently feel later.

Let's face it. Relationships **are** difficult to manage – at least to manage well. The trouble we have in relationships, inside and outside of work, can often be traced back to how we manage (or mismanage) the Equity Equation. As a manager/leader, you will face four challenges in trying to manage equity in the relationships with the people who work with you. You've got to meet and beat them all.

Challenge 1: Building Trust
Challenge 2: Hidden Expectations
Challenge 3: Stamp Collecting
Challenge 4: Using The Wrong Psychological Currency

Let's take them one at a time.

Challenge 1: Building Trust

Trust, of course, is important in all relationships, but it's especially crucial between you and the people who report to you. If you don't have it, you're going to get nowhere fast. Several years ago, researchers at The Center for Creative Leadership identified the chief causes business executives fail in their organizations. At the very top of their list were arrogance and insensitivity to other people. Running a very close second was not being trustworthy.

Are *you* trustworthy? If you are like most people, based on a scale from 1 to 10 (10 being the most trustworthy), odds are that you consider yourself to be between a 7 or an 8. Now, using that same scale, as a whole, how trustworthy do you consider other people to be? The typical responses we hear to this question are 4, 5, or 6.

How does this relate to your job? A survey by researchers at Boston University found that 80% of employees in organizations simply don't trust top management. Unfortunately, in terms of the Equity Equation, trust is an Outcome we expect from others in our relationships but an Input we are reluctant to provide for them.

Why? Well, let's start with some of your own biases. Assume that you believe that trustworthy people tell the truth and keep their word. Now make a mental list of occupations you see as being untrustworthy. How about used car salespersons? Mechanics? Politicians? Journalists? Lawyers? Given a little time, you probably could fill out a very long list. One reason we have trouble trusting others is our assumption is that they will take advantage of us, lie to us, cheat and steal from us, in order to get what they want from a relationship.

An executive headhunter once told us what he thought was his most valuable interview question: "Would you lie?" He said that anyone who said "No" was already lying. When the response is "Yes," he then probes to find out why the person would lie and to describe the circumstances in which they would be dishonest. One CEO candidate, when put to that test, answered, "Absolutely not!"

"Why not?" the interviewer asked.

"Because I've got a lousy memory," the candidate replied.

Another reason trusting others is difficult is that trust in relationships does not come about quickly. When beginning a new relationship, we tend to withhold trust until others prove that they can be trusted. People have

To be trusted is a
greater compliment than
to be loved.

– George MacDonald

to earn our trust just like they have to earn our respect and friendship. New employees are less likely to be given access to confidential company information than are senior employees who have already justified our confidence in them. Thus, we refuse to trust other people who simply say, "Trust me." Our position is, "Show me first that you can be trusted!"

The final problem is that trust is very fragile, like a piece of fine china. Building a relationship based on trust can take a very long time, but smashing it can take only seconds. One simple violation of trust shatters whatever trust has been built, and we then suspect that the person can't be trusted at all, ever. Once our trust has been violated, we usually aren't willing to give that person a second chance. If we do, we do it very grudgingly.

So, how can you build and maintain trusting relationships with others at work? Trust, like all human attributes, is based primarily on perceptions not necessarily reality. There are three essential qualities in a work-oriented relationship on which trust is constructed:

- How ***competent*** people think you are.

- How ***caring*** people think you are about others.

- How ***dependable*** people think you are in being both caring and competent over time.

Building Trust

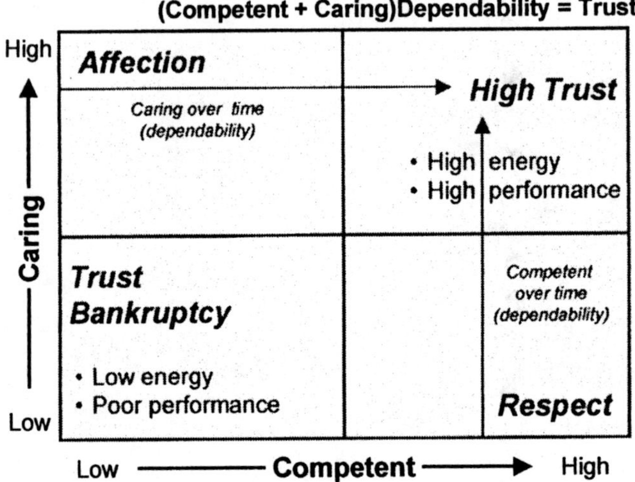

Depending on how people perceive your combination of competence and caring, you may find yourself in one of four types of trust relationships:

- Relationships based primarily on **Respect**
- Relationships based primarily on **Affection**
- Relationships in **Trust Bankruptcy**
- Relationships based on **High Trust**

Here is a guide to each one of these types of trust relationships.

Relationships Based On Respect: If people see you as being very competent at your job but caring little or not at all about people, you probably will earn the respect of those around you, but not their trust. Many of us have known people who are great at their jobs, but whose attitude toward people is so cold and indifferent that we can't bring ourselves to trust them. Indeed, some of us have known very competent people that we would trust only as far as we could throw them. But merely being competent can only gain you respect – it won't necessarily cause your people to trust you.

Relationships Based On Affection: If you are perceived as highly caring of others, but not perceived as very competent at what you do, those you work with may think of you affectionately as a friend or a kind person, but they won't necessarily trust you on the job. Caring for people may gain you affection, not necessarily trust. If are a leader in this kind of relationship with your employees, they'll think kindly of you, they'll enjoy your company, but they won't think enough of your judgment to consider you much of a leader. In short, they'll think of you as a pleasant bumbler, nothing more.

Relationships In Trust Bankruptcy: If the people who work for you don't see you as being either caring or competent, then your relationship with them is in trust bankruptcy. As a leader, your effectiveness in your relationships with the people who work for you is at great risk because there is simply no foundation on which to base the relationship (we will discuss more about trust bankruptcy in the next section).

Relationships Based On High Trust: If you are perceived by people to be both highly **competent** at your job and genuinely **caring** about people – and you are able to demonstrate these two qualities again and again over time (i.e., you are perceived as **dependable**), then you are well on your way to building high trust relationships with your employees. As a leader, *high trust* relationships are the foundation to fostering *high performance* work relationships.

Putting the Trust/Performance Relationship to Work For You

Think about one of your relationships at work. Which of the following levels of trust characterizes that relationship?

Trust Level I

High Trust = Spontaneous Behavior

When a high level of trust exists, people show little concern about getting their share from the relationship. They feel confident that the other person will not take advantage of them. The mode of behavior at this level is for both parties to take from and give to the relationship spontaneously.

A high trust relationship is a high energy, high performance relationship.

Trust Level II

Low Trust = Cautious Behavior

People in low-trust relationships are preoccupied with equity. People at this level behave in ways that secure their fair share from the relationship while at the same time seeing to it that the other person doesn't gets any more than their fair share as well. The mindset is "I'll do this, if you do that."

A low trust relationship is a low energy, low performance relationship.

Trust Level III

Trust Bankruptcy = Aggressive/Passive Behavior

When there is trust bankruptcy (i.e., mistrust) people may engage in one of two totally different behaviors:

Aggressive: People in trust-bankrupt relationships can seek to exploit the other person. They withhold Inputs and try to maximize Outcomes. The mode of behavior becomes "Get the other guy before he or she gets you."

Passive: The second reaction is quite different. People simply withdraw from the relationship or break away from it completely. When there is no trust, they avoid contact with the other individual in the relationship, ask for a transfer or just quit to find another job.

A trust bankrupt relationship results in little to no performance because all energy is focused on attacking the other person or on strategies to exit the relationship.

Think about your reactions when trust diminishes. You feel defensive and worry about being taken advantage of. You start figuring out how to "Get them before they get you." While it's true that trust creates trust, distrust brings defensiveness and an "I win, you lose" relationship orientation. And when you've trusted someone else and they've disappointed you, your resentment and anger lead easily to the words... "I don't get *PAID* enough for this!"

Challenge 2: Hidden Expectations

You might recognize the old riddle:

> *A father and his son are driving to work one morning. A terrible accident takes place. The father is killed instantly and the son is badly injured. An ambulance rushes the son off to the hospital emergency room. He is taken quickly to surgery. The on-duty surgeon walks in, looks at the boy, and says, "I'm sorry. I can't operate on him. He's my son."*

How can this be? The father was killed in the accident. You might guess that one father was a stepfather or perhaps a priest. Maybe the son was illegitimate or adopted. There are many possible explanations.

This simple riddle illustrates the concept of hidden expectations, the second reason why equity in relationships can be tough to manage. These expectations are products of our past experiences from childhood to present day. Perhaps your experiences tell you that most surgeons are male. And that's why you can't break through your own hidden expectations and determine that the surgeon in our riddle was actually the boy's mother.

These expectations are hidden for two reasons. First, people often don't realize how such expectations influence their own behavior. Second, even when they are aware of these expectations, too many people simply don't communicate them to others. Either way, hidden expectations slumber along, dormant, nudging the ways in which we act very subtly until some relevant event sets them off.

- An older plant manager, raised during tough economic times, is enraged to discover that he can't get his younger-generation hourly employees to put in overtime. "In my day, I would have been damned happy to grab the overtime pay," he thunders.

- A new employee is troubled. She's just received a warning for showing up at the job a few minutes past 8 a.m. In her previous job, workers had some flexibility as to when they would show up and leave, as long as they put in a full day's work.

A manufacturing executive recently explained to us an incentive system his company created after hearing a never-ending torrent of complaints from hourly workers about their wages. The system offered cash incentives for any worker who exceeded management-set production quotas. The system worked. As soon as it was instituted, productivity leaped by nearly 20 percent. Was the executive happy? Not in the least. He confided to us that this sudden burst of productivity confirmed his worst suspicions. "For all these years, I just knew these people were goofing off and not really putting in a full day's work," he said.

Hidden expectations often influence how you treat people in organizations. Think about the first person you ever supervised. You probably poured a lot of energy into making sure this person did the job right, carefully explaining what you expected, giving ample feedback and feeling genuinely responsible for the person's success. Then, over the years, as you supervised more and more people, you might have communicated less and less. You might have figured that all the people you supervised after the first one had that same person's strengths, and you were quietly surprised or even disappointed when they did not.

Too often people don't perform because we simply don't tell them what we want. We unintentionally keep our own expectations hidden from them. Study after study reveals that most people can't even summarize in a sentence or two what their job is technically supposed to be, let alone explain the more informal expectations their bosses have of them.

Thus, past experiences – in jobs and other relationships – build expectations about how people should behave. When we as managers/leaders keep these expectations hidden, our employees aren't really sure what we expect from them. When they don't or simply can't conform to our expectations, both parties can feel cheated and are convinced the Equity Equation is loaded in the other person's favor.

Challenge 3: Stamp Collecting

Maybe you're familiar with the trading stamps shoppers used to collect as a bonus for shopping in supermarkets and department stores. People pasted these stamps into little books, and when the books were filled, they could redeem them for toasters, clocks, even vacations. In work relationships, we "collect" and "redeem" stamps as well, but usually the results aren't nearly as pleasant or productive.

One manager told us about her "stamp" collection on her boss. During the five years she worked for him, he did a lot of things to help her complete her stamp book. When they went out for lunch, he'd frequently be in the restroom when the check arrived. He would tell visitors to park in her parking place. He frequently took credit for her ideas and work. He often bypassed her and dealt directly with the people who reported to her. He made nasty jokes about women managers and insulted his own boss behind the boss' back. All during that time, the woman manager was mentally collecting her stamps of her boss' inequitable treatment and consideration of her.

Then, it was time to cash in the stamp book. She caught him falsifying an expense report when he claimed he'd taken a trip he'd never made. "I'd probably have turned him in anyway," she said, a smile playing on her lips. "But after all he'd done to me, I got an extra dose of satisfaction out of seeing him clean out his desk after they fired him." She was able to trade in her stamp book for a sense of justice and her Equity Equation tipped back into balance.

There are more productive ways to deal with problems than stamp collecting. One obvious one is to confront others when they irritate or upset us. But we fail to do so for several reasons. First, we are inclined to give others what psychologists call *idiosyncratic credit* – credit that allows important people in our lives to behave in eccentric, idiosyncratic, and bothersome (to us) ways. In this way, we try to overlook their irritating behavior by telling ourselves that the relationship itself is more important. But as we collect more and more stamps, their credit runs out.

The Mum Effect

In organizations, people collect stamps because they are victims of what is called the **Mum Effect**. Mum is an acronym that stands for **M**um about **U**ndesirable **M**essages. Few people enjoy being the bearer of bad news, especially subordinates. The boss of our stamp-collecting executive was a victim of the Mum Effect. Each time she chose not to speak up and confront her boss, she added another stamp to her collection until her book was all filled up and she decided to redeem it against him.

Divorcements

Stamp collecting has subtle signs, including engaging in divorcements. No, that doesn't mean quitting in a door-slamming huff or throwing a transfer request on the boss' desk. **Divorcements** are when employees begin to distance themselves from a work relationship in subtle, often unseen ways. Maybe they start showing up for work late, use up their sick days, take longer and longer lunch hours and other breaks. Each divorcement is nothing more than an effort to balance the inequity they feel with every stamp they collect.

Divorcements are one reason people don't always end work relationships over just one issue. Instead, they withdraw a little each day, counting their stamps, holding their grudges and magnifying their anger. The event that pastes the final stamp in the book may be trivial. But, big or small, when the final incident pastes the last stamp in the book, they cash it in. And what are they thinking when they do? "I *really* don't get PAID enough for this!"

Challenge 4: Using The Wrong Psychological Currency

How much is one dollar worth? A dollar will probably buy you the same cup of coffee in California as it will in Florida. The exchange rate is the same on the East and West Coasts. When you travel to a foreign country, the exchange rate is usually fixed as well. One dollar will get you approximately 10 pesos, 2 marks, 7 francs, 120 yen, and so on, depending on the exchange rate that day. In our economic transactions, the currencies are tangible and the rate of exchange is fixed.

In work relationships, we exchange “currencies” as well. But most of these relationship currencies – especially when they apply to the Hidden Paycheck – are not tangible and the exchange rate is rarely fixed.

Remember Harry, the stressed-out executive who expected to be promoted as a reward for all the long hours and hard work he had given to the company? When his coveted promotion went to someone else, what he got instead was, at least from his perspective, a slap in the face. His boss told him that Harry seemed so overwhelmed with the work he already had that taking on a new assignment was too much for him. So, they decided to offer the job to someone who could handle it better.

Harry's boss is like many other leaders. They think their decisions are firmly rooted in what's best for the people who report to them and the company. What they discover too late is that what their people were really looking for was something else entirely. Though these leaders are well meaning, they end up using the wrong Psychological Currency.

The reason equity in work relationships is difficult to manage is that the currencies we provide – our inputs to the relationship – are either misunderstood or not appreciated by the other person because they are simply the *wrong* currencies.

Remember the list you made of your Inputs and Outcomes for an important work relationship you have? Go back to page 63 and look at the list. Are your certain that the other person in the relationship actually values the Inputs you listed? The truth is this person may actually think that you're giving only a fraction of what you think you are, or that what you're giving is unimportant.

Take a look at these examples:

- An employee gets to work 30 minutes early each morning and stays 30 minutes after quitting time in order to complete an important project before her deadline. Her boss, instead of telling her what a great job she's doing, blows up at her for accumulating so much overtime.

- An executive thinks raising people's pay can solve his company's morale problems. After he gives a significant across-the-board raise, he's frustrated when his problems don't disappear in a "puff of green smoke."

- A manager treats her employees warmly and considerately. Even so, the people who report to her don't respect her because they think she doesn't have the backbone to fire some people on the team who aren't doing their share of the work.

Unfortunately, there are countless examples in which people who poured lots of effort into making what they consider important contributions to a workplace relationship found out that the other party didn't value or appreciate what they had contributed.

The ~~Golden~~ Platinum Rule in Relationships

One reason we often give the wrong psychological currency is that we have learned to apply the golden rule faithfully:

Do unto others as
you would have them do unto you.

Here's the problem. What we want from others may not be what they want from us. A better prescription for making sure people feel they're "getting as good as they giving" is an approach we identified in 1989 and which we and others have dubbed the **Platinum Rule**:

Do unto others as
they would have you do unto them.

So, before you pour your time, energy, creativity, planning and other currencies that you consider valuable into a relationship, think about the kinds of currency the

The 20 Outcomes People Want From Work

System Outcomes

- Pay
- Fringe benefits
- Promotion and advancement
- Job security
- Working conditions

Job Outcomes

- Using one's abilities
- Challenging work
- Decision making
- Responsibility
- Meaningful work

Performance Outcomes

- Accomplishment
- Achievement
- Competence
- Personal worth
- Confidence

Interpersonal Outcomes

- Belonging
- Recognition
- Status
- Appreciation
- Job friendships

The Secret of
THE HIDDEN PAYCHECK

other people in that relationship might value. Once you understand what's important to them, you'll know what kind of currency people are looking for from their Hidden Paycheck.

What Employees Want From Work

During the past ten years, we've identified 20 important Outcomes people typically want from their jobs. We've classified these 20 Outcomes into four categories:

- System Outcomes
- Job Outcomes
- Performance Outcomes
- Interpersonal Outcomes

You as an immediate manager/leader will have varying degrees of influence over System or Job Outcomes. Most of us, though, no matter what our position in the organization, have considerable impact on the Performance and Interpersonal Outcomes of our direct reports.

These 20 Outcomes, with the exception of pay, can also be grouped under another name: **Hidden Paycheck Currencies.** These are the currencies people are looking for from their work that are beyond the scope of their regular paycheck. These are precisely the currencies that you, as a leader, can provide to your employees to impact their performance. Taken together, these currencies **ARE** the Hidden Paycheck.

Over the years, we have surveyed thousands of people in a wide range of industries and positions. We have asked each of these people to rank order these 20 Outcomes as to which ones are actually most important to them. Here is a list of the top 5 Outcomes people say they want from work. From top to bottom, they are:

Top Five Outcomes People Want From Work

1. A sense of accomplishment
2. Recognition for good work
3. Competitive pay
4. Making use of their abilities
5. Challenging work

For many of us, these are the "right" psychological currencies that we want to be paid in. Surprise. You probably saw that "Competitive Pay" was in the middle of this pack. It's certainly important, but it only came in at #3. A sense of accomplishment and recognition for good work actually ranked higher in terms of what people really want from work.

Now think. Hard. How many jobs actually give people an abundant amount of these Outcomes/Hidden Paycheck Currencies? When your employees are calculating their own Equity Equation, figuring out what they give to the company and what they get back based on these currencies, then that's what you've got to give them. You may think that great pay or a whopping bonus ought to be enough to motivate your people to leap tall buildings for you. But that's not how they always see it. And if you're not paying them the currencies they value, then they won't much care about what you want.

The flip side is the shiny side. If you do give them the kind of currencies they want, they'll do a better job for you and be more productive than you could ever have imagined.

So, now that you know that, in addition to pay, there are many other things your people want from work, you need to know how you can go about delivering what they want. You're about to learn how to actually payout the Hidden Paycheck.

The deepest principle in human nature is the craving to be appreciated.

– William James

Chapter 8
Paying The Hidden Paycheck To Your Employees

When our working relationships with direct reports aren't going well – when employees aren't performing the way that we need or want them to – we often tend to feel a bit helpless. Why? Because we focus on what the other person is or is not doing. We think that *they* are the problem and we tend to focus almost exclusively on the *their* behavior. It's what the other person does or does not do that helps or hurts the relationship. From this perspective, we all like to think that the world would be a much better place if everyone else did things more like we think they should do them.

Your point of view starts to change, however, when you start thinking about how you can manage your work relationships through the Equity Equation. When you look at your workplace relationships through the equity lens, you may see that many people, including some of the ones who report to you, feel they're giving a lot more than they're getting. They feel Under-Rewarded. You might not agree with their perceptions but, basically, that doesn't matter. What matters is how your employees perceive the relationship. Period. Perceptions are all that count in relationships.

However, that's no reason to start feeling helpless. You've got a lot more control than you think in your relationships with the people who report directly to you. How? You have power over:

- How other people "see" what they're putting into the relationship.
- What other people actually "get" out of the relationship.
- How other people "perceive" what they're getting from the relationship.

Put simply, you as the immediate manager/leader have the power to influence how people perceive their Equity Equation at work. There are five ways for you to do it. We call them **Hidden Paycheck Payoffs** (**HP Payoffs**, for short). You can use each and every one to pay your people their Hidden Paycheck. Here they are:

HP Payoff 1: Changing Perspectives
HP Payoff 2: Promoting Positive Expectations
HP Payoff 3: Setting Goals
HP Payoff 4: Providing Performance Feedback
HP Payoff 5: Offering NRBs (Novel Rewarding Behaviors)

The rest of this chapter will discuss each HP Payoff in detail. You'll see how using these HP Payoffs can help rebalance the Equity Equation for your employees. When you deploy these five methods, you'll start getting the high performance you want and need – now and into the future.

HP Payoff 1: Changing Perspectives

Maybe you've read the poem about the six blind wise men who had heard about elephants but had never experienced the real thing. One day, they decided to call on an elephant. But because they were all blind, they couldn't actually see the elephant. So, each wise man decided to touch the elephant to determine what the animal was like. Here is what they concluded:

- The first stumbled into the elephant's side and decided that an elephant is like a wall.

- The second touched the elephant's tusk. He compared the elephant to a spear.

- The third held the elephant's trunk and concluded that elephants are similar to snakes.

- The fourth felt the elephant's leg and decided that elephants are much like trees.

- The fifth, holding the elephant's ear, stated that elephants are very much like fans.

- The sixth, grasped the elephant's tail and claimed that all elephants are like ropes.

The poem concludes...

And so these men of Indostan,
Disputed loud and long.
Each in his own opinion,
Exceeding stiff and strong.
Though each was partly in the right,
And all were in the wrong.

We, too, can be like the six blind wise men when it comes to relationships. Like the blind wise men, each person may see the world from a very different point of view. As you know, there are three viewpoints that are at work in the Equity Equation – your perception, the other person's perception, and the facts. People often feel they're giving more than they're getting at work because they have blinders on their perceptions. Like the wise men groping randomly to try and learn about elephants, we become so consumed by the way we perceive things that we can't see or understand others' points of view or reality.

Differing ways of defining equity result from people having differing points of view about Inputs and Outcomes in a relationship. However, you have both the power to recognize and change the perspectives of those who work with you. A shift in perspective can do a lot to restore equity in a relationship.

When you first were introduced to the Equity Equation earlier in this book, you learned that psychologists and others really don't know how people judge the Inputs and Outcomes in their life. Sometimes we compare what we give and get to what other people like us (including coworkers, friends and peers) appear to give and get. Sometimes we compare what we give and get to another relationship we've had in the past (be it a previous job, marriage, etc.). Sometimes we compare what we give and get to what the other person in the relationship (a boss, subordinate, spouse, etc.) gives and gets. There are many ways to analyze the situation. But, no matter where a person's comparative standards come from, these comparisons are how they determine whether they're getting equity in a relationship.

So what standards do you use to evaluate your pay? Previous raises? Coworkers? Your efforts on the job? Your spouse's salary? It might be a little of all four. Just as you have your standards for deciding if you are paid well, so other people use their own perspectives and standards to evaluate their Equity Equation on the job.

Remember, the people reporting to you have a little mathematician inside who is furiously calculating how much they are giving to the job in relation to what they think they are getting in return. Remember, each person is using his or her own personal formula to make these calibrations, even if it's not the most accurate one or the one you would use.

That's where you come in. As a manager/leader, your role is to help your people see things from a point of view they may not have used before. Just by changing their perspective, you can offer them a brand new way of assessing their Equity Equation with you and your company.

Listening for Perspectives

You can identify other peoples' perspectives simply by listening to them describe why they feel they're Under-Rewarded. Sometimes their point of view may strike you as being a bit silly, but it's their perspective that matters and you have to take it seriously.

A bank manager recently told us about her astonishment when a subordinate complained that his new desk was too small.

"I don't understand the problem. It's the same size as the desk of every other loan officer here," she explained to him.

"I know that," the subordinate replied, emotion edging his voice. "But it's a smaller desk than my secretary has and I do more work than she does."

Laughing inside, the manager had the bank buy the subordinate a credenza, a supplement that seemed to satisfy the subordinate, though the manager wryly wondered to herself if she should have just made him do his secretary's work for a few days instead.

Sometimes just listening to people can affect their point of view. A major reason workers feel they're giving more than they're getting is that they feel nobody knows or really cares about what they do. Consequently, they think nobody has any idea about the vital contributions they make to the team and the entire organization. What better way to change the way people look at their Equity Equation than to listen to them?

By the way, listening can't just be some kind of placating gesture on your part. If your people feel they are giving more than they are getting, you can't do anything about that perspective until you know what it is. The only way you'll find out how a person looks at their personal Equity Equation on the job is by getting them to describe it for you and listening, really listening, to what they have to say.

The Power of Perspective

Once you know the way other people look at things, you also have the power to manage and even change their point of view. For example, a colleague gave us this letter from a college student to her parents:

> *Dear Mother and Dad,*
>
> *Since I left for college I have been remiss in writing to you. I am really sorry for my thoughtlessness in not writing before. I will bring you up to date now, but before you read on, please sit down. You are not to read any further unless you are sitting down. Okay?*

Well, then, I am getting along pretty well now. The skull fracture I got when I jumped out of the window of my dormitory when it caught fire shortly after my arrival here is pretty well healed. I spent only two weeks in the hospital, and now I can see almost normally and get those sick headaches only once a day.

Fortunately, the fire in the dormitory (and my jump) was witnessed by an attendant at the gas station near the dorm, and he was the one who called the fire department and the ambulance. He also visited me in the hospital, and since I had nowhere to live because of the burnt-out dormitory, he was kind enough to invite me to share his apartment with him. It's really just a basement room, but it's kind of cute.

He is a fine boy, and we have fallen deeply in love and are planning to get married. We haven't set the exact date yet, but it will be before my pregnancy begins to show. Yes, Mother and Dad, I am pregnant. I know how much you are looking forward to being grandparents, and I know you will welcome the baby and give it the same love and devotion and tender care you gave me when I was a child.

The reason for the delay in our marriage is that my boyfriend has a minor infection, which prevents us from passing our premarital blood tests, and I carelessly caught it from him. But I know that you will welcome him into our family with open arms. He is kind and, although not well educated, he is a hard worker. I know your often-expressed tolerance will not permit you to be bothered by that.

Now that I have brought you up to date, I want to tell you that...

There was no dormitory fire.
I did not have a skull fracture.
I was not in the hospital.
I am not pregnant.
I am not engaged.
I am not infected.
And there is no boyfriend in my life.

However, I am getting a D in History and an F in Biology, and I wanted you to see these grades in their proper perspective.

Your loving daughter,
Susie

Obviously, the Susie who wrote this letter pulled back her sleeves and tried to work some major perspective magic on her parents. Altering perspectives can be a very powerful tool for the leader trying to manage equity. But Susie's letter also demonstrates the most important element in changing someone else's point of view – communication.

Communicating to Change Perspectives

When you're responding to the way other people see things, you might, in fact, conclude that they are indeed not getting as much as they're giving. If that's the case, the only way to restore equity is to increase their rewards. But if they really aren't being shortchanged, then you can help them to see things differently. Here are two ways:

1. First, you can change the way they look at what they're putting into the relationship. Employees who feel they're not getting enough recognition and reward for what they contribute might need to see their efforts differently. You can help them see their contributions (Inputs) in light of one or more of the following:

    - Other people's efforts
    - Their own efforts on previous projects
    - Their own skills and ambitions
    - The actual results of their efforts
    - The increased expectations brought on by a recent change in responsibilities

2. You can change the way they look at what they're getting out of the relationship. Some people need to see the recognition and rewards (Outcomes) they're getting in light of:

- The recognition and rewards other people get
- The future recognition and rewards they might receive compared to the ones they're getting now
- The recognition and rewards they received on previous projects
- The expectations other people have for rewards and recognition

In short, you need to help other people take the blinders off their own perspective and look at a bigger, or even different, picture.

The Constraints of Limited Perspective

Can you run a four-minute mile? Probably not. Most people can't. Being able to run that fast probably isn't very important to you. However, for some people, being able to run a four-minute mile is at the top of their lifetime achievement list. Since the time of the ancient Greeks, running fast has been a highly prized ability. The Greeks tried lots of ways to get people to run faster – even having lions chase runners in order to make them run faster! Not too surprisingly, the lions often won, making running a rather hazardous profession in ancient Greece.

Even now, the spectacle of runners racing around a track can make hearts pound all over the world. The question of who really is the fastest human being on earth is an enticing one. Over the years, one track and field event has captured the special fascination of spectators, the one-mile race.

At one point in the late 1800s, when the world record for the one-mile race was around 4.15 minutes, speculation began as to who would break the four-minute mile. For decades, runners trained, strained and stretched themselves to the utmost to break that four-minute barrier, with no luck.

People started to believe that humans weren't physically capable of running that fast. Experts testified that anatomically, our bone structure and lung capacity weren't up to the task. These so-called limitations, plus numerous other human physical shortcomings, all seemed to conspire to make the four-minute mile an unreachable goal. Many runners came within a gnat's eyelash of achieving the impossible, but all of them failed, and the legend of the achievement's impossibility mushroomed. It even took on a title: "The Four-Minute Barrier." And that's how people saw it. It was a great wall that you could come close to touching but could never break through.

Everything changed on May 6, 1954, when 25-year-old, British runner, Roger Bannister, crashed through the barrier and ran the mile in 3:59:4 minutes at Oxford. People worldwide were stunned, convinced that it had to be a fluke or a miracle. Well, whatever it was, it soon reached epidemic proportions. The same year that Bannister crashed through the barrier... so did 37 other runners! The following year, more than 300 runners ran a mile in less than four minutes.

Think about this for a minute. For hundreds of years, nobody could run a four-minute mile. Then, after one person did, more than 350 other people were able to do the same thing within the next 18 months. What happened? Did humanity suddenly take a huge evolutionary leap forward in 1954? No, probably not. However, the way people looked at the four-minute barrier took a huge leap. A leader set a new standard by achieving what previously had been considered to be impossible.

Roger Bannister's feat (no pun intended) allowed runners all over the world to expand their perspective. Once they began looking at a four-minute mile as within their grasp, runners from all over the world began to perform better than they or the thousands of runners before them ever had. And the momentum hasn't stopped yet. The current world record for the mile is 3:43:13.

Maybe you can't run a four-minute mile, but you, like Bannister, can set new standards. By getting your people to change their limiting perspectives, you can help them achieve levels of performance they never thought possible.

No doubt you're a little skeptical right now, and you have a right to be. But know this: A few years ago, in a one-mile race in New York, all 13 runners in the race finished in times under four minutes. The person who came in dead last, who trailed every other runner in that race, still achieved what people had thought impossible only a few years before. That's the power of freeing people from a limiting perspective.

HP Payoff 2: Promoting Positive Expectations

In the late 1700s, an Italian professor invented a cure for toothaches – simple and guaranteed to work for a full year. Suffering patients were told to crush a worm between their thumb and forefinger. Not just any worm, but one known by its Latin name as *Curculio antiodontaligious*. Then the patients were told to apply the worm's remains to the problem tooth and the pain would vanish. Suspicions of quackery soon arose. A special commission was appointed to determine the truth of the Italian's claims. The commission, after grilling hundreds of toothache patients, found that almost 70% of the people who had used the Italian's cure said their tooth pain had surrendered to the power of the worm.

Maybe you're smiling at this old story of mind over matter. Remember, though, that the professor's patients expected a cure, and they got one. This small story illustrates a large lesson in human behavior: People who expect to succeed generally do. The flip side is also true. People who expect to fail will have their expectations confirmed as well.

Why mention this bit of psychology at all? Because, as a leader and manager, another power you have is the power of positive expectations.

How Positive Expectations Work

The idea that your expectations can influence the behavior of others had existed for centuries. Perhaps you have heard of the Pygmalion effect. The original Pygmalion was a mythological king who carved an ivory statue of the ideal woman. He named the statue Galatea. And because she was so lifelike and so beautiful, Pygmalion fell in love with her. His belief in Galatea, so the story goes, caused Aphrodite, the goddess of love, to bring the statue to life.

George Bernard Shaw based his play Pygmalion on this myth. It is the story of a professor who tries to change a flower girl into a proper lady. The power our expectations have on the behavior of others is reflected in lines spoken by the play's main character, Eliza Doolittle:

> *The difference between a lady and flower girl is not how she behaves, but how she's treated. I shall always be a flower girl to Professor Higgins, because he always treats me as a flower girl and always will; but I know I can be a lady to you, because you always treat me as a lady, and always will.*

The Pygmalion Effect is an example of what is also called the self-fulfilling prophecy, a powerful but simple principle: if you think something is going to happen, then it will.

A friend once told us how a self-fulfilling prophecy helped him avoid becoming seasick. He'd heard on a radio talk show that when some doctors go deep-sea fishing, they put a tiny adhesive bandage behind one ear before setting off. This adhesive bandage somehow affects the inner ear's balancing mechanism, the talk show guests said, thus warding off seasickness.

A few months later, our friend went on a family vacation and had a chance to go deep-sea fishing. He and his father-in-law secured some adhesive bandages from their hotel's kitchen. To make doubly sure that the cure would work, they each placed a bandage behind both their right and left ears. Our friend told us that despite the boat's constant lurching, and the inelegant view of their fellow passengers throwing up over the boat's side from seasickness, he and his father-in-law had their lines out all day. They munched on candy bars and apples, feeling absolutely no effects of the rolling sea. They even cured the seasickness of a young newlywed on the boat by sharing their adhesive bandages with her.

More than a year later, our friend learned accidentally that some doctors do indeed wear adhesive bandages behind their ears while deep-sea fishing – but the bandages are soaked in *scopolamine*, a prescription drug for motion sickness. The drug is slowly released through the skin, slipping into the bloodstream, warding off any symptoms of seasickness. Our friend was astonished. He and his father-in-law had dodged the nausea just by using the bandages, with no drug whatsoever. His story was another illustration that if people believe something will happen, it will.

That's what you, as a leader and manager, have to accomplish. By having positive expectations of the people who work for you, you plant a self-fulfilling prophecy in their minds. A slew of studies have proven that creating positive expectations profoundly affects the performance of other people – and for the better.

Positive expectations work for two reasons.

1. They alter perspectives by combating the negative expectations many people carry around, like overloaded baggage, from one working relationship to another. This dead weight is the leftover inequity from bosses who didn't treat them fairly, organizations who fired them, etc. But, your having positive expectations for these people will change their outlook from "I can't succeed " to "You bet I can succeed and I can start right now."

2. The second reason positive expectations work is that when you communicate these expectations to others, you are at the same

time giving Outcomes – Hidden Paycheck Currencies – to them.

Let's explore both these reasons for a few minutes.

Combating Negative Expectations

First, you have to accept that most people carry negative expectations around with them, like garbage in a huge gunnysack. In fact, many of us tend to think more bad about ourselves and the world than good. We're hardwired to expect the worst, not the best.

So, imagine you're at a banquet with 99 other people. You've finished the meal, the servers are clearing away the dishes, and the banquet is coming to a close. As the toastmaster completes her announcements, she says, "And now for the special surprise. When you entered the room tonight, we wrote each of your names on a slip of paper. The box in front of me contains all one hundred names. I'm going to shuffle these papers around, then draw one. The person whose name is on that slip will win a $10,000 cash prize."

You now have two options:

- *Option 1:* Stand up and move toward the podium. The toastmaster is sure to draw your name.

- *Option 2:* Stay in your seat and say to yourself, "It probably won't be me. My chances are only one in a hundred and I never win these things anyway."

If you are like most other people, you chose the second option. Realistically, your chances of winning are only one in one hundred. Realistically, you also have absolutely no control over whose name the toastmaster will pull from the box. Since you are now in such a realistic mood, let's change the scenario slightly.

You are kidnapped by some terrorists and are taken prisoner in some far-off country. There are 99 other prisoners in there with you. It's about lunchtime, and the chief guard strolls into the room, scowling. His voice booms out: "I've got some bad news for you. We've got enough food for only ninety-nine people. So I've written each of your names on a slip of paper. All of the names are in this box. I'm going to stir up the names and draw one out. If I draw your name, we're going to take you outside and shoot you."

Again, you have two options:

- *Option 1:* Stand up and walk to the door. The guard is sure to draw your name.

- *Option 2:* Stay in your seat and think, "It probably won't be me. My chances are only one in a hundred and I never win these things anyway."

The irony in this illustration is that the odds in both situations are identical – one in one hundred. The amount of control we have is the same – none. Yet most of us think we'll get the bullets and not the bucks.

So, what can you do to neutralize the negative expectations that we all tend to cling to so dearly? It's not as tough as you think. Consider the following illustration provided by one of our colleagues.

Our friend's first graduate school course was statistics, a subject most students anticipate with the same glee as they would a trip to the dentist for a root canal. To add to his stress, our friend had always done poorly in math. In college, he'd taken only two math courses, and he'd had to repeat one of them. Not surprisingly, he entered his first day of the course thinking, "I'll never be able to wade through this stuff. I wish I didn't need this class to graduate."

Then the class began. The professor listed all the course assignments, and then strode over to the blackboard. He picked up a piece of chalk and for the next twenty minutes, the professor practically covered the entire blackboard with one long mathematical equation. Fear gripped our friend's throat. His stomach felt queasy. This was his first message from the alien world of statistics.

The professor then turned to the class and boomed out: "This equation will be on the final test. Memorize it."

Our friend thought he was going to faint.

Then the professor gently laid down the chalk and turned to the entire class, hundreds of students, all virtually paralyzed by fear. He smiled.

“I know a lot of you are worried about surviving this class. But if you can add, subtract, multiply and divide, then you can do statistics."

Our friend claims that he can still remember the sighs of relief (mostly his) that swept through the classroom. He also remembers that, as it turned out, there was much more to statistics than basic math. The professor had stretched the truth a bit that first day. “But by the time I found that out,” he said, “I was doing so well it just didn’t make any difference.”

The power of positive expectations you build in other people can and does lift the weight of negative expectations that people carry around with them. You, as a manager/leader, do have impact over what kind of expectations your people choose to envision for the future. And these positive expectations are actually some of the Hidden Paycheck Currencies your employees are so desperately searching for.

The Outcomes of Positive Expectations

Picture yourself and a friend having lunch one sunny afternoon. Your friend looks up from his salad and says, "I've got a tournament this Saturday."

"What kind of tournament?" you ask.

"Horseshoes," he responds, his mouth a little stuffed with greens. "I'm the state horseshoe pitcher champion."

"Wow! I didn't know you played horseshoes, and I sure didn't know you played that well."

"Yup. In fact, I'm heading out to practice right after lunch. Wanna come along?"

"Sure, but I haven't played in years."

"That's okay," your friend says, smiling a very big smile. "Let's just play for fun."

Delighted at the prospect of having a new kind of amusement, you drive your car behind your friend's out to a horseshoe pit. As you step out of the car, your friend opens his trunk and pulls out a black leather briefcase. He lays it on the hood, then snaps open the lock. The case is lined with foam, and in two U-shaped cutouts are a pair of chrome-plated horseshoes. Each one is engraved at the top with your friend's initials.

He unpacks the horseshoes and you both walk over to the pit. Your friend takes two warm-up tosses. Both are ringers. He retrieves the shoes, hands them to you and asks, "Ready?"

"Guess so," you reply uncertainly. "But it looks a lot tougher than I remember."

"It is tough. And, just looking at you, I'm not so sure you're coordinated enough to pitch very well anyway."

With that kind of encouragement, not only might we question the friendship, but most of us would ask ourselves in some desperation, "What am I doing here?"

Now, let's put this scene on rewind. Assume your friend has taken his warm-up tosses and handed you the horseshoes. Then, when you say it looks a lot tougher than you remember, he replies, "It is tough. But I can tell just by looking at you that you'll be one dynamite horseshoe pitcher." Wow. With that one simple sentence, look at what your friend has given you.

Outcomes of Positive Expectations

1. A sense of competence
2. A feeling of personal worth
3. Status
4. Belonging
5. A sense of confidence

When you let people know that you have positive expectations of them, you give them some great Outcomes – Outcomes they get even before they do anything.

That's how positive expectations work. When you give people positive expectations, you help them overcome the baggage they carry around with them from the past. Positive expectations give people a sense that they will get something good from this relationship. Positive expectations replace the hidden, negative expectations people carry around inside of them with clear expectations that they will perform well.

You can deploy positive expectations in any number of situations with the people who report to you. You can use them with new hires on their first day, people who are trying hard to accomplish difficult tasks, transfers into a new position under you, or people who just need a good psychological lift. Just find a way to say to them, "Just looking at you, I think you'll turn out to be one dynamite horseshoe pitcher."

Equity Expectation Meetings

So, when is the best time to start setting expectations with your employees? The best initial opportunity you have is right after they are hired and join your team. It is the perfect time to sit down and discuss what your expectations are of them ***and*** learn what their expectations are of you, the organization, and their new job. We call this an Equity Expectation meeting. Remember, many times the reason people want to join your team is that their expectations were not met at their last job.

The key to Equity Expectations meeting is having both parties engage in *empathic listening*. One special version of empathic listening requires that each person articulate his or her expectations and then listen as the other person repeats those expectations back to them. Empathic listening has the listener:

1. Listen attentively.

2. Repeat what they think the other person said.

3. Ask the speaker to verify if their understanding is correct.

It is a relatively simple procedure that provides confirmation to the person communicating that the other party is actually understanding them.

When most of us speak, it is not just to hear the sound of our own voice. It is important that we know that the person we are talking to is both hearing and understanding what we are trying to say. By engaging in empathic listening during Equity Expectation meetings, you are verifying that your employees understand what you expect of them and, even more importantly, you as the immediate manager/leader, understand what they expect from you, their job, and the company.

Of course, Equity Expectations meetings are the perfect time to start setting lots of positive expectations for everyone all around.

The First 40 Hours

The initial Equity Meeting is crucial. For new employees, the strongest perceptions of their new manager and the organization will be etched into their mind during the first 40 hours on the job. During that time, we form important perceptions about whether we made the right choice in taking the job and we lock in on what's important to our immediate manager and the organization. As the immediate manager/leader, you have to be especially alert to how you interact with your newest team members. Remember, always try and focus on positive expectations.

But as important as the first 40 hours are, don't confine expressing positive expectations and having Equity Expectation meetings to the first 40 hours a new person joins your team. You can't afford to pretend these expectations drop off a cliff after that. You have to check back with your people now and then. Expectations evolve and change over time for yourself and for the people who report to you.

If you don't keep their equity expectations and yours up-to-date, then you'll find yourself making blind stabs at what your people want from you, and they'll be trying to decipher what you want from them. You have to have very clear positive expectations articulated both from yourself and each person who reports to you. If that doesn't happen, then both of you are groping in the dark and the Equity Equation becomes very difficult to manage.

A Word of Warning About Positive Expectations

By themselves, positive expectations are powerful incentives to perform well. However, they cannot guarantee performance. If you build positive expectations in others who nevertheless fail, then they may blame themselves, and you, for their failure – one more entry for their stamp collection. The only thing worse than not having positive expectations is to have them but fail anyway. To give everyone a chance for success, explore some other HP Payoffs. These Payoffs are designed to keep other people's expectations of themselves in the positive range. The more positive your people are about their own ability to contribute, the more likely it is they'll succeed.

HP Payoff 3: Setting Goals

Each morning, millions of people drag themselves out of bed and force themselves out the door and into work, dreading the day ahead. They plod through the next several hours doing just enough to keep their paycheck coming in and their boss off their back. When quitting time rolls around, they zip out to the parking lot, leap into their vehicles and launch themselves like guided missiles away from their jobs, their bosses and their organizations.

Where are they going? Someplace they want to be, to do something they want to do. Maybe it's to play golf, tennis, bowling, or softball. Maybe they want to go to the gym or have a round of drinks with their buddies. Or go play with the kids. Why are they suddenly so energized? Because they have a goal: They have a place they want to be and they have something they want to do.

A goal. Sounds like something very small, but for most people, it looms large. How long would fans watch football if the goal posts and yard lines vanished? How long would people flock to basketball games if the baskets disappeared? How long would you garden if nothing grew? People enjoy these activities because they give them something to shoot for. The sad thing is that we do a much better job of creating goals for our life outside work than we do in our jobs.

Literally hundreds of studies have shown what you probably already know: people with goals perform better. So why aren't people in organizations performing any better than they are? How come nearly 85% of employees say they could perform better if they wanted to? Yes, remember that statistic? Eighty-five percent of

American workers said they could do more work, and more than half said they could double their productivity, if they "wanted" to. Why don't they "want" to? Because they don't have strong, focused goals they can relate to at work.

We know that setting goals works. But we have to do it right in order to make sure people feel they're getting as good as they're giving at work. Goals can be set in one of three ways:

- "Do Your Best" Goal Setting
- Assigned Goal Setting
- Participative Goal Setting

Some methods work and some of them don't. Let's see why.

"Do Your Best" Goal-Setting: Why It Doesn't Work

"Do your best" is one of the most popular ways to set goals in many organizations. Common sense would say that just asking people to do their very best would be enough, but common sense would be wrong. Think about it for a moment, and the reason will become clear. More specifically, think about the kinds of things you like to do when you're away from work.

Maybe it's golf, tennis, running or even fishing. Well, they've all got specific goals attached. For example, we once asked a golfing buddy what his handicap was. "My swing," he wryly replied. Actually, he has a 15 handicap and is working mightily to get it down to 10. Other golfers simply struggle to break 100. But, they all have a goal.

Tennis players have their own goals during a match. These include making sure their serves and returns stay in bounds and clear the net. Almost all will say they want to win. People who fish want to land the illusive "one-that-got-away." Runners work to improve their times. Across this country, family rooms, recreations rooms, bedrooms, and sometimes garages are cluttered with trophies and other mementos of individual and group exploits in goal achievement.

So think for a few minutes about why you enjoy those off-the-job activities. And check your reasons against the list of Outcomes of specific goals you see below.

Outcomes of Setting Specific Goals

1. Challenge
2. Using one's abilities
3. Meaningful work
4. Making decisions
5. Responsibility

If you play golf, there's the challenge of trying to break 100, or to hit every green in regulation, or to shoot par.

And the goal also brings many problems to solve, such as getting out of the woods or a sand trap. Tennis players enjoy competition with others and the game calls for their best athletic abilities. Runners feel personally responsible for improving their times and make decisions about how fast or slow to run at different points in a race. The Outcomes received from goal setting cause our performance to improve.

Remember when your horseshoe-playing buddy said that he thought you'd make a dynamite horseshoe pitcher? And how good you felt? You got an Outcome, in this case a shot of confidence, even before you started playing. People also receive Outcomes even before they get in the game. Why? Because these Outcomes focus their desire and efforts to succeed.

Having no specific goals is like being on a ship without a compass. You don't have a clear idea of where you're going or how you're going to get there. If you tell someone to "just do your best" and they produce only three-fourths of what you expected, you'll be disappointed and your employee may actually think he or she had achieved a lot. And if the next time out that person achieves only three-fourths of what was done before, you'll be even more frustrated – and the employee won't know what the problem is.

So, forget "Do-Your-Best" Goal-Setting. It's the easiest way to set goals, but it preserves one of the worst aspects of many workplace relationships: hidden expectations which don't get communicated until after there's a problem. This brand of goal setting doesn't pay off in any Hidden Paycheck currency either. It offers no Outcomes that give people a sense that they're getting as much as they're giving.

Assigned Goal-Setting: Why It Doesn't Always Work

By now, you probably think that if you just set specific goals for people that they'll have something specific to shoot for and there won't be any problem figuring out whether the goal's been achieved. True enough. But how do you go about calculating how high or low the goals should be?

It's easy when we set goals for ourselves. Maybe it's saving $10,000 to invest, losing 20 pounds, or paying off all your credit cards. When we're setting goals for ourselves, we have a real good idea of whether we can achieve them. However, when it comes to setting goals for other people, we don't always know enough to be able to figure out what the right goal is for them. Not convinced? Take a 10-minute break and try this exercise:

1. Take out a blank sheet of paper.

2. Write the words "RHODE ISLAND" on top of the page.

3. Now make a list of 30 words out of any combination of letters in the state's name. Remember, you've only got 10 minutes, so work fast.

How'd you do? You probably got 30, because almost everyone does. When you reached that goal, you achieved the Outcomes that people generally get from reaching specific goals. Note that a sense of accomplishment, the most important Outcome that people want from their jobs, is at the top of that list.

Outcomes of Achieving Specific Goals

1. A sense of accomplishment
2. Feelings of personal worth
3. Achievement
4. Sense of competence
5. Status

Some people get to thirty words in less than four minutes. And then they usually quit working. If we had set your goal at forty, you would have most likely made that goal, too. The result would have been a 33% increase in production. As you can see, the results of setting goals too low can limit the amount of effort you would put into attaining a specific goal.

Then there's the flip side: setting goals too high. Goals that are almost impossible to reach simply frustrate people, and they give up. When we've used the "RHODE

ISLAND" example in our workshops, we sometimes will say that the goal is 100 words. One person out of 40 will reach this goal. Others will just abandon ship at 15 or 20. They quickly realize that they can't make the goal and give up. By setting goals too high, you can actually *take away* Outcomes people are looking for.

A university president once told us about how her father used high goals to push her toward success in grammar school. She still remembers greeting him at the front door when he came home from work one evening. Filled with pride and pleasure, she showed him the results of her spelling test.

"See, Dad! I made a ninety-eight," she said, beaming.

Her father paused, looked at the grade and asked. "So who made the one hundred?"

Her father's strategy is one a lot of managers and leaders use. During a recent economic downturn, one department store chain decided it would improve its sales through a goal-setting program. When commissioned salespeople opened their weekly pay envelopes, they found computerized notes attached to their checks. Here's a sample:

> *During your last pay period, you produced $10,000 in sales. Your quota for the next pay period is $12,500.*

At first, the sales force leaped at the chance to strut their stuff by meeting the challenge of this 25% quota increase. Sales shot through the roof that first week. But with their next paycheck, they once again got a 25% quota increase over their newly increased sales. Again, they rallied to the task. About three pay periods into the program, the salespersons grasped that the quotas were becoming impossible to meet. Even worse, the harder they worked, the more impossible the quotas would become, because the quotas were being ratcheted up 25% each week.

They rebelled. Under enormous pressure from a resentful and angry sales force, the chain's management aborted the program. Sales immediately slumped to pre-program levels. Management, however, had shot itself in the foot. Not only did resentment continue to smolder over the abandoned program, but the sales force now also suspected any future attempts to set goals as being little more than management manipulation.

Assigned goal setting does provide a target for people to shoot for, but it works only if you know what your people are capable of achieving. Perhaps you're familiar with IBM's 100% Club. Membership is limited to IBM salespeople who have made at least 100% of their sales quota for the previous year. Interestingly, about four out of five IBM salespeople belong to the club. Why? Because management has set challenging but attainable goals. That means 80% of the company's sales force is meeting the goals, joining the club and collecting the rewards (Outcomes) that well-gauged goal setting can offer.

However, if you're not sure what your people can actually do and you set the goals too high, you'll have a bunch of resentful people who feel they aren't getting as much as they're giving. And if you set the goals too low, then you'll be getting less from them than they can give. That means productivity and performance are less than they could be, and that's not good for them, you or the company.

So, if you don't really know what your people can do, then what's your alternative? The answer is participation.

Participative Goal-Setting: Why It Works

Participative goal setting means that you allow people to help set goals for themselves. They participate in the process. Participative goal setting ensures that goals are realistic – that people who work hard can actually attain them. That's only one of its advantages. There are two others as well.

- First, people who set goals for themselves often set higher goals than the goals you would have assigned to them. An important exception is people who feel severely Under-Rewarded. They may tend to set goals low enough to put you out of business. But on the whole, you will end up with better and higher goals when people set their own.

- People who set goals for themselves work harder to reach them because they "own" the goals. The goals belong to them, not you. That means they'll be a lot more committed to making sure they will achieve what they themselves said they could.

Whoa. We know what you're thinking. Participative goal setting doesn't mean simply turning people loose to amble around and decide on their own what they're willing to do. Nope. You play an important part. As their manager/leader, you will talk to your people and help them choose their goals. You and they will agree on what they realistically can do, then you will let their ownership of those goals and their commitment to achieving them do the rest.

Remember, you've already seen ten psychologically important Hidden Paycheck payoffs specific and realistic goals can provide. If you use participative goal setting, then you're adding an 11th payoff – you're demonstrating a trust in their ability to help manage themselves and their relationship with you. So, by all means, give them something to shoot for. Just let them help pick the target.

In short, participative goal setting gives your people specific, realistic goals that you and they have agreed upon. Because these goals produce so many Hidden

Paycheck payoffs, you are helping your people *and yourself* make sure that they feel they're getting as much as they're giving.

There's a second benefit. This kind of goal setting makes sure that hidden expectations about how other people should perform get tossed out the window. Whether it's an individual employee working to boost her sales by 10% during the next quarter, or an entire division trying to stay under budget, goal setting brings your expectations into the open, where everyone can see them and know what they are.

One last point here. Goal setting isn't something you have to reserve for a quarterly meeting. You can use it every day. The next time someone asks you when you need a report finished, don't say something vague, like "Oh, anytime next week." Instead, ask that person when it can be done. After discussing it, you can both agree that, for example, Tuesday at 5 p.m. will be fine.

Okay. We started out our discussion about how to pay your people the Hidden Paycheck in your work relationships by saying that you have a lot more control than you might think over how they see their Equity Equation. We hope you're coming to realize that managing relationships effectively is, in part, a matter of helping people understand and change the way they look at their workplace relationship.

It's also a matter of giving important Hidden Paycheck Payoffs to others by communicating with them directly. You also have to make sure you listen as well as talk.

Let's look at that aspect in a little more detail.

HP Payoff 4: Providing Feedback on Performance

It was his first circus. His grandfather had promised to take him on his next birthday, and now they were there. The smells of cotton candy and peanuts tickled his nose. He was mystified by the astonishing feats the circus animals performed. He watched wide-eyed as the elephants knelt down and rolled over like his dog, then stood majestically on their hind legs. His head bobbed as the horses trotted in line around the center ring, while riders jumped on and off the horses' backs at will. But his mouth popped open and his eyes bulged as a huge male lion leaped fluidly about a caged ring, climbed a ladder, crept along a narrow board suspended nearly 15 feet in the air, then jumped through a large, flaming hoop.

He tugged on his grandfather's sleeve and whispered excitedly, "Grandpa, grandpa, how do they get the lion to do that?"

"Do what, son?"

"How do they get the lion to jump through the hoop when it's on fire?"

The old man looked down and smiled at his grandson. "Well, it's like this. They go out in the jungle, set a hoop on fire, hang it from a tree, and wait. They capture the first lion which jumps through the hoop and bring it back to the circus."

The boy's brow knotted. "Is that really how they do it, grandpa?"

"No, not really. They actually go out into the jungle and look for a lion, preferably a young one. Then they catch him, bring him back to the circus, and train him," the grandfather said,

Then the grandfather, who knew something about these matters, explained the whole process. How, when the lion first begins training, a hoop which is not on fire is placed on ground level in a ring. The lion walks around the ring, and eventually walks through the hoop. As soon as he does, the trainer gives him some meat. When he walks through the hoop again, the trainer gives the lion more meat. Pretty soon, the lion figures out that going through the hoop means lunch.

As the grandson listened intently, and the "ooohs" and "aaaahs" of the crowd surrounded them, the grandfather explained that, bit by bit, the trainer raises the hoop, and the lion learns he has to jump through it in order to get more meat. Soon the hoop is 15 feet high. Most lions can't jump that high, so they have to climb a ladder and edge along a catwalk so they can get to the hoop.

The grandfather paused to sneeze. After he put his handkerchief back in his pocket, he explained that it was at this point that the trainer set the hoop on fire.

"Fire scares lions, of course," he said, glancing out at the center ring, where a lion was jumping through another flaming hoop. "But they crave fresh meat even more. So the lion learns that jumping through the flaming hoop earns him a lot more meat, and he's willing to do it. It's a lot easier than going hunting in the jungle."

The boy paused, looked out at the center ring, then turned to his grandfather. "But, Grandpa. Why does the lion tamer keep cracking the whip like that?"

The old man chuckled. "That's just for show, my boy. The lion could care less and his master knows it."

You're probably not in the business of taming lions, though you may sometimes feel like it when you're trying to manage relationships on the job. But this story has two morals:

- People (lions, too) perform better in relationships when they get feedback on their performance.
- People perform better in relationships when the feedback they get is positive.

Think again about the things you like to do when you're off the job. One reason you like these activities is that they give you something to shoot for. Most of them also give you feedback about your performance. You see what happens when you hit a golf ball, serve a tennis ball, watch your garden grow, land a striped bass or hear the sound of your favorite musical instrument when you play it.

At work, though, we often don't get feedback. Instead, we have to wait until someone tells us how we're doing. Too often, we think the wait will last forever – unless the feedback is negative. Then we hear about it right away.

In many organizations, we lead by exception:

If you don't hear from me, that means you're doing OK. But make a mistake, and I'll climb down your throat.

Using this kind of management, leaders do crack the whip and it's not just for show. When, for example, was the last time you called a meeting to give someone a pat on the back for doing something right? When was the last time you sat down with your team to list all the things that they do well?

Negative feedback, a verbal kick in the rump, is simply a form of punishment. When people get negative feedback, they often want to give less, not more, to you and to the organization. That's not good. Sometimes, though, you've got to give negative feedback. Later in the chapter, we'll show you how to do it productively.

In the meantime, though, if you emphasize positive feedback, letting people how well they are doing, you'll be surprised at how rarely you need to use negative feedback when managing work relationships. When you give your people positive feedback, you also pay them many Hidden Paycheck currencies (Outcomes).

Outcomes of Positive Feedback

1. Recognition
2. Feelings of competence
3. Sense of accomplishment
4. Status
5. Appreciation
6. Confidence
7. Feelings of achievement
8. Personal worth

These payoffs build equity, so your people feel they're getting more and more for what they're giving. From this sense of equity comes, and, by now, you shouldn't be surprised, much better performance. But you've got to give feedback well, or it won't work.

Qualities of Effective Positive Feedback

If you believe in the power of positive feedback, then you'll probably recognize the four qualities that make positive feedback work. Feedback should be:

1. Immediate
2. Specific
3. Tied to performance
4. Genuine

Let's take a look at each of these qualities in more detail.

1. Feedback Should Always Be Immediate: When you whack a golf ball on the golf course, you know almost instantly how far down the fairway (or into the woods) it's going to travel. In tennis, the ball is either in or out. And when you bowl, you actually get to see the pins fall.

Unfortunately, the only feedback many people get is at performance review time. That could be once every three months, six months, a year or even longer. One company actually schedules these ego-threatening events on the employee's birthday!

In most jobs people do don't get the kind of immediate feedback they do when playing golf or tennis. That's where you come in. As the manager/leader, part of your job is to give frequent feedback, especially when employees are doing something that doesn't in itself give an immediate feedback. Feedback is so essential that it's at the core of numerous management-training programs for business leaders at every level within organizations. Still, we can't help but wonder whether all of this training actually helps.

For example, nearly 15 years ago we developed a survey to see how well managers and their subordinates were communicating. Consider the following statement managers find on the survey.

I Let My Subordinates Know When They Are Doing A Good Job

Managers have to choose an option that shows how often they actually do this. Here are their choices. Pick one for yourself:

Always	Frequently	Occasionally	Seldom	Never
☐	☐	☐	☐	☐

If you picked Always or Frequently, then you responded the same way more than 3,000 other managers throughout the country answered. In fact, on a scale of 1 (never) to 5 (always), the average response for managers is 4.3. Judging from their own point of view, managers are doing a pretty terrific job of giving their subordinates feedback for work well done.

Hold on. We then presented the following statement to a representative sample of the subordinates for those 3,000 managers:

My Supervisor Lets Me Know When I'm Doing A Good Job

We also asked them to pick one of the following five options as to just how often their supervisor gave them positive feedback. Pick the one that pegs how often your own supervisor tells you that you're doing a good job:

Always	Frequently	Occasionally	Seldom	Never
☐	☐	☐	☐	☐

Ooops. If you're like the nearly 11,000 people at all levels of the organization who have responded to our survey, you didn't choose Always, or even Frequently. One the same 1 to 5 scale, the average score is only 2.3! We have dubbed this canyon-sized chasm – where managers give themselves 4.3 for giving feedback and their subordinates score them at a measly 2.3 – **The**

Feedback Gap. That's a nearly 200% difference between what managers think they provide in terms of positive feedback and what subordinates actually register. And, remember, their perception is their reality!

The facts would probably say that the truth is somewhere between 2.3 and 4.3. But the only perception that counts is the one which produced the 2.3 score. When employees say they don't get much feedback, and, whether true or not, it's a perception in need of repair. In your relationships with the people who work for you, you need to face this fact: They probably think you don't give nearly as many pats on the back as you think you do. And, you can't afford to wait until these people quit or get promoted to ask, "Did I give you enough feedback?" No, you've got to address this situation squarely and immediately. If you want to manage relationships effectively, then catch your people in the act of doing something right. Then tell them so. Right away.

2. Feedback Should Be Specific: Specific feedback tells people exactly how they did. In many of our recreational activities, it's really easy to know how we did. Bowlers can see how many pins were knocked down, golfers can see how close the ball is to the cup. Relationships are a lot more vaporous. When people do give pats on the back, they're usually wrapped in generalities like, "You're doing a great job," or "Thanks for the good work."

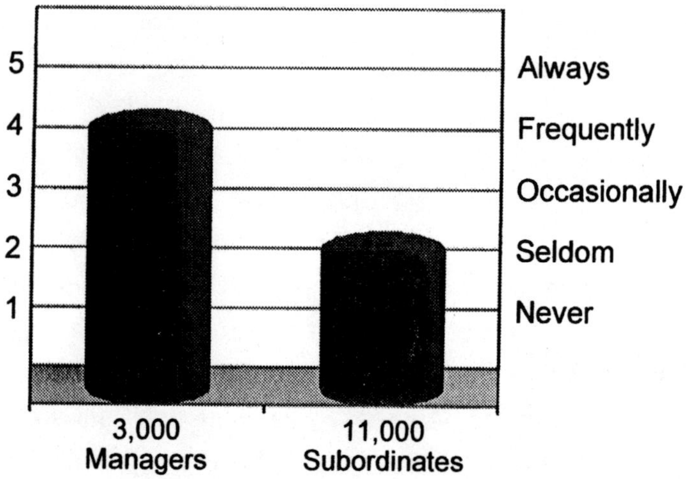

The Feedback Gap: A 200% difference between the amount of positive feedback managers say they give and the amount of positive feedback subordinates say they get.

That's not to say you shouldn't pay general compliments to people. But specific statements have a higher payoff in Hidden Paycheck Currencies than general statements do. They also buttress people's continuing to do what you want them to do in the way you want them to do it. Tell people that the way they did a specific job was terrific and they're likely to do it that way again. Suppose, instead of saying, "Great job," you said any (maybe even all) of the following:

- "Thanks for getting this report done so fast."
- "I'm really impressed by the way you were able to pull the information together so quickly."
- "It's great to have someone I can count on to keep a cool head when we have tough situations."

People, including you, want recognition for their unique contribution to relationships. They want to stand out. That's why organizations have forms of recognition such as Employees of the Month, Million-Dollar Round Tables, and 100% Clubs. Specific feedback lets people know that you recognize how special their contributions actually are and that you have noticed and prize the talents and qualities they bring to their relationship with you and the organization.

3. Feedback Should Be Tied To Performance: Effective feedback is not just immediate and specific. It also is tied directly to performance. Some years ago a consulting firm marketed a wristwatch with nine stems, a real one and eight dummies. The dummy stems were all painted red, and all anyone could do with them was to pull them out or push them in.

The idea was for managers to wear this watch in the morning with all eight dummy stems out. Then, between 8 a.m. and 9 a.m., the manager would approach one of his or her subordinates and say, "You're doing great work for us. We really appreciate it." Then the manager would walk away, punching in one of the dummy stems. The ritual would be repeated each hour. By day's end, the manager would have given eight pats on the back, timed by the red reminders on the manager's wrist.

The watch was helpful because it reminded managers to give feedback to their subordinates. Maybe this approach seems corny or silly, but many managers who get caught up in other matters during a day desperately need reminding to give their employees feedback on their performance. However, this watch device had a major flaw. The pats on the back were tied to time – one per hour – not to a subordinate's actual performance.

Just going around giving people a cookie-cutter thank you doesn't work. If positive feedback isn't pegged to something specific the employee has done, then it is nearly worthless for the employee. The employee may even see it as an empty, even manipulative gesture, rather than a sincere attempt to give praise.

Of course, the other problem with the wristwatch approach is that it didn't take into account whether the employees actually were doing a good job. The wristwatch only encouraged managers to give praise often, not just when it was deserved. The critical issue here is that as a manager/leader, you have to give the people who report to you feedback that is immediate, specific *and* pegged to real performance. Which boils down to this: Be genuine. Which is what we're going to discuss now.

4. Feedback Should Be Genuine: Some people have told us they don't like the wristwatch approach because it's too gimmicky. They're probably right. Lots of gimmicks work, but probably not that one. It prompts managers to dish out praise, not because it's deserved, but simply because it's time to do it again. Employees aren't stupid. They can tell when you're faking it. If they think your praise is insincere, they won't think much of your pat on the back, or of you, for giving it.

Look. You want people to be genuine with you. You have to return the favor. For many leaders, though, giving praise feels awkward, and your awkwardness can come off as being insincere, even if you're not. The solution is simple. Practice, practice, practice.

If you want to be a person who gives genuine feedback, then do exactly that. Over and over. After a while, doing it will become a natural part of your relationship with the people who report to you, and probably others as well. If you give pats on the back routinely and tie them to performance, your employees won't have any doubt about how genuine they are. If you make giving sincere praise as much a part of your day as putting on your shoes in the morning, then people will see it as a natural part of what you bring with you to work. Any possible mistrust of your sincerity will evaporate.

To recap, positive feedback works when you:

1. Give it right away

2. Make it specific

3. Tie it to performance

4. Make it genuine

This kind of four-fold feedback is extremely potent because it gives employees loads of the Hidden Paycheck payoffs they want from their work. With those payoffs comes an increased sense of getting a lot for giving a lot. People get an increased sense of equity. And with more equity, you'll find people do better work.

The Dilemma of Giving ~~Negative~~ Developmental Feedback

Sometimes, though, you have to give people negative feedback. Part of your role as a manager/leader is to keep people from doing things you don't want them to do.

However, feedback doesn't have to be negative. Instead, it can be ***developmental***. The difference between the two is simply the difference between being constructive and destructive. Developmental feedback makes a person aware that one of their *behaviors* is inappropriate and is designed to prevent that *behavior* from occurring again. Negative feedback, on the other hand, usually doesn't target the inappropriate behavior(s), but rather makes a person feel that they are being criticized or belittled.

Some years ago, management expert Douglas MacGregor outlined what he called the Hot Stove Principles of Punishment. All of us learned early in life that if we put our hand on a hot stove, our hand will get burned. The resulting pain of this action is severe enough to remind us never to intentionally do it again. From this analogy, MacGregor developed several principles that can be translated and applied to other forms of "punishment."

We've adapted MacGregor's principles here to give you five guidelines for giving developmental feedback to your employees to prevent them from repeating behaviors that are undesirable.

Guideline 1: If you touch a hot stove, you get burned right away. In work relationships, our reaction to undesirable behavior is not always immediate. Many leaders wait days, even weeks, to tell an employee that they're unhappy about something the employee did.

Sometimes leaders put off this unpleasant communication so long that the employee doesn't have a clear idea what the punishment is for. As we have said before, effective positive feedback should be immediate. Effective developmental feedback should be, too. If you need to do it, do it on the spot.

Guideline 2: The hot stove punishment is intense the very first time you touch it. At work, we tend to give developmental feedback fairly gently the first time around. If it happens again, then we're likely to be a little more harsh. If it happens again, we use even stronger punishment. That's the wrong approach. If your developmental feedback is appropriately intense the first time, you probably won't have to repeat it.

Guideline 3: The hot stove punishes only the hand that touches it. When you touch the hot stove, your whole body doesn't get burned, only your hand. When giving developmental feedback to employees, we often get too personally involved, sometimes to the point of losing our temper. So, instead of focusing on the behavior, we end up punishing the entire person. The focus of developmental feedback should be on changing the specific behavior(s) a person is engaging in that are inappropriate. You're not trying to squash the entire person. If you keep your objectivity and focus only on the specific behavior(s), then your feedback will have a much better chance of affecting only those behaviors, not the whole person.

Guideline 4: The hot stove is universally consistent. No matter whose hand touches the hot stove, the hand gets burned. At work, we're sometimes tempted to punish one person for acting a particular way, but to let other people doing the same thing just slide by. Don't do this. This kind of inconsistency makes people wonder what their leaders really want or whether they're playing favorites. You can't afford to have people who work for you wondering about either situation. Your reaction should be consistent, no matter whose behavior it is that needs to be changed.

Guideline 5: If you touch a hot stove, you have ways to stop the pain. If your hand hurts when you touch the hot stove, you can move it and stop the pain. Sometimes at work, leaders punish the way someone is acting, but don't say what these people should have done instead. Bad move. For developmental feedback to work, people need to know what they ***should have done*** or what ***they can do*** to avoid the hot stove again.

If you think through these five guidelines and apply them the next time someone is behaving in a way that is inappropriate, you'll have a much better chance of snuffing out the problem before it becomes a major issue.

But, and this point can't be stressed enough, you'll be far better off using positive feedback frequently. Use developmental feedback only when necessary. Indeed, using positive feedback will cut down on the number of times you have to pull out your developmental feedback skills. People would much rather know when they're doing something right, but too often we simply don't tell them and just end up cooking them on the hot stove.

Goal Setting + Feedback = Performance[2]

The HP Payoffs you're seeing here work well individually, but they are most effective when used together. In particular, setting goals and giving feedback will produce performance far above using either one alone.

Some Stanford University researchers studied several groups of soldiers who were competing for coveted spots in special units. The soldiers had undergone weeks of arduous training and they had only one more challenge to face: a forced march in full gear. Motivation for the teams was very high. The soldiers knew that if they weren't able to keep up, they would lose their chance to be assigned to one of the special units.

The soldiers were divided into four groups. The groups would have no communication with one another during the march. Each group would march 20 kilometers (about 12.5 miles) over exactly the same terrain on the same day. Each group, however, received different instructions before starting their respective march.

- Group 1 was told the exact distance they would march (the 20 kilometers) and received frequent feedback about their progress along the way.

- Group 2 was told only this. "This is the long march we've been telling you about." They had no idea how far they'd have to go, nor did they get any feedback about their progress while they marched.

- Group 3 were told that they were going to march 15 kilometers. After marching 14 kilometers, they were told that they had another six to go.

- Group 4 were told they had to march 25 kilometers and, again, after 14 kilometers, they were told they only had six more to go.

Before you find out how the groups did, which one do you think did the best, and why?

Of course, Group 1 did the best because they knew exactly how far they had to go (they had a specific goal) and were regularly informed as to how well they were doing while they were moving toward the goal (they received frequent feedback which created a sense of accomplishment).

Group 2 turned in the worst performance. The idea of undertaking "that long march we've been telling you about" without any notion of how long it would be or how well they were doing along the way, gave them no specific goal to strive for and the lack of feedback didn't offered them any sense of accomplishment.

How Goal Setting and Feedback Affect Performance Levels

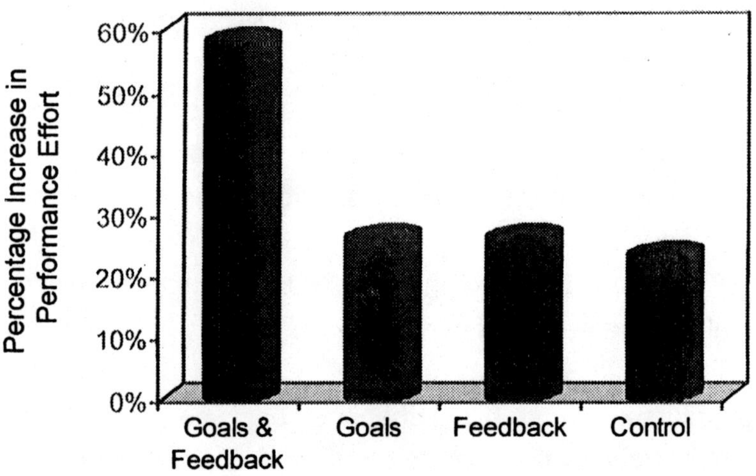

The real surprise was Group 3. They came in second despite being told to march 15 kilometers, then being told at the 14-kilometer mark that they actually had another 6 to go. Apparently, the group was so highly motivated the extra distance didn't daunt them.

Group 4 finished third. Why? One possibility would be that once they heard they didn't have to march the original 25 kilometers they'd been told, and that they actually had only 6 kilometers, not 11, to go, they may have lost some of their motivation to meet their first goal.

Interestingly, the researchers also measured stress levels for each group. The results were very similar to the order in which they finished. Blood tests were taken during the march and 24 hours afterward. The blood was tested for cortisol and prolactin, hormones that increase with stress. Group 1, which knew exactly how far it had to go and how it was doing, had the lowest stress levels. Group 2, had the highest stress levels, probably because it had no idea how far they had to march, only that this "is the long march we've been telling you about" and got no feedback on their progress. Groups 3 and 4 fell in the middle in terms of stress levels.

What can you as a manager/leader get out of this study? If you give your people a combination of goal setting and feedback, you could dramatically increase their performance as well as keep their job stress to a minimum.

HP Payoff 5: Offering NRBs (Novel Rewarding Behaviors)

Many organizations give rewards, perhaps a five-year gold pin, then an emerald-and-gold pin for a 10-year employee. If someone works for the company 20 years, then maybe diamonds will find their way into that pin. These rewards, however, are based on a single factor – survival. The message is:

Survive the job, your boss and the company,
and you'll get another reward.

These time-honored traditions have their uses, but too many companies are inhabited by people who are merely survivors, not winners. That's a shame. Too many people never get a taste of what it's like to be a winner. The power of novel rewarding behaviors – those things we do for employees that are both pleasant and unexpected – is to celebrate winners rather than those who merely survive.

Some years ago, an executive we know was appointed to the presidency of a large commercial construction company. When he took control, the company was nearly bankrupt. One of his first acts was to sign a contract with a large corporation for his company to build an office building in 13 months at a cost of $23 million. When he signed that contract, he knew he couldn't do the job within 13 months. Nor would $23 million begin to cover his company's costs. But he needed the business, so he took his chances.

But he also did a lot more. Late one evening, he visited the construction site to check on the building's progress. The foundation was being laid, and he noticed something striking. Some workers had laid cement blocks, the main components of the foundation, nearly eight feet high. Other workers across the construction site had built their blocks only three or four feet high. Obviously, some people were performing well, and others were barely crawling along, doing marginal or, at best, average work.

The president walked to his car and took out some envelopes and paper. Then he walked back to the construction site. As he passed the areas where people had met or exceeded his performance expectations, he stopped and wrote a note that simply said, "Thanks for doing a great job." Then he took a twenty-dollar bill from his wallet, wrapped it inside the note, put the note and the money in the envelope, and left it there. That night he spent almost $400 of his own money. But it was worth it. As he later told us, "You should have seen people laying cement blocks the next day."

This event wasn't a one-time quirk. The president rewarded both quality and quantity of performance on that building in other unexpected ways: catered lunches, T-shirts, decals for hard hats, more cash bonuses, and even on-the-spot pay raises for exceptional work. In total, he spent $48,000 on novel rewarding behaviors while the building was being constructed. But his people finished the building two months early and for almost $100,000 under the contract price.

Today, this executive is still president of the company. He also owns it. And when he negotiates contracts for office buildings, he insists that the contract price include money to pay for his novel rewarding behaviors program. In return, he can assure buyers that they're getting a quality building which will be completed on time and on budget. He's a genuine winner, but his employees are, too. Being showered with novel rewarding behaviors (NRBs for short), means that he's showing his people that he recognizes and appreciates their high-quality performance.

Outcomes of Novel Rewarding Behaviors

1. Recognition
2. A sense of accomplishment
3. Status
4. Personal worth
5. Appreciation

NRBs at Work

Unlike our construction executive friend, you don't have to spend thousands of dollars to begin an NRB program. Of course, $48,000 was pocket change compared to what he got in return. But here's a list of NRBs which don't cost much but that enrich your relationship with your people and can help make spontaneous winners out of survivors:

- Afternoons or days off
- Personal thank-you notes
- Achievement decals for hard hats, badges for uniforms and T-shirts.
- Tickets to sporting or cultural events
- Gift certificates to restaurants or day spas

This list is barely a beginning of possible NRB's you could use. Most likely, you can think of even more and better ways to reward your employees.

A Word of Caution

At work, NRBs can help boost the egos of everyday survivors and make them feel like winners. But there are some yellow caution flags to consider as you ponder ways to use NRBs:

- Be sure you're using the right currency for your employees. Not everyone will appreciate a T-shirt, or a ticket to a ball game.

- Don't forget that NRBs should be spontaneous. If you take employees to lunch two birthdays in a row, the novelty will wear off. What's worse, they might come to think of the birthday lunch as part of their benefits package.

- NRBs, just like positive feedback, should be tied directly to the performance of the team or an individual employee.

Regardless, NRBs are powerful ways to offer significant Hidden Paycheck payoffs to your employees. And, as we've said before, the richer the Hidden Paycheck, the better the performance.

Now you know about the five Hidden Paycheck **Payoffs** you can offer your people.

HP Payoff 1: Changing Perspectives
HP Payoff 2: Promoting Positive Expectations
HP Payoff 3: Setting Goals
HP Payoff 4: Providing Performance Feedback
HP Payoff 5: Offering NRBs (Novel Rewarding Behaviors)

Using these five major Payoffs can make you a better leader/manager by giving you the ability to rebalance the Equity Equation with your employees. You can give them more of what they want from work so that they, in turn, give you more of what you need from them. But, as powerful as they are, don't think for a minute the Hidden Paycheck is limited to just these five HP Payoffs.

<u>The REAL Secret of the Hidden Paycheck</u>

You see, the beauty of understanding the Equity Equation – really understanding it as the bedrock of the

Hidden Paycheck – is that you'll find yourself giving Payoffs to your people in lots of different ways that we didn't even mention here. When Give-To-Get Leadership becomes second nature, you'll find yourself, quite naturally, thinking about give-to-get in all of your interactions with your employees.

For example, you might see that offering your employees some personal flexibility in their schedules so that they can go to a doctor's appointment or accompany their child to a special event, will not mean you will get less performance, but more. You will see that by simply putting an acknowledgement into a report thanking the employees, by name, who contributed to it will mean more to them than any tangible reward ever could. The point is that the Hidden Paycheck can be paid in innumerable ways.

When you really understand the concept of Equity and why Give-To-Get Leadership works, you have in your grasp the most powerful formula for influencing human behavior on the job – and off.

These Give-To-Get techniques work. All you have to do to know just how well they can work is to lean back, close your eyes, and imagine just how much more satisfying and productive your own work life would be if your boss started paying you your Hidden Paycheck. But, for now, you're the one who has to deliver the payoffs, not receive them. We think you'll be very pleased with the results.

Chapter 9
Putting It All Together: The Leader As Coach

Choosing to pay your employees their Hidden Paycheck is a big decision. The ideas we have presented in this book may be a complete departure from what you are used to in your current organization or from your experiences in the past. Leaders who recognize, understand and can effectively manage the Equity Equation are few and far between. As we have said from the beginning:

N	*O*	*T*	*E*
V	*E*	*R*	*Y*
O	*N*	*E*	*W*
I	*L*	*L*	*G*
E	*T*	*I*	*T* *

However, we want to add one final piece that can really help you maximize the power of the Hidden Paycheck. It requires you to rethink the way you look at the role you play with your employees and what it really means to be a leader.

Have you ever been part of an athletic team? Have you every had a personal trainer help you get physically fit? How about worked with a music coach to fine-tune your performance? And, of course, some of you may have

** Again, the secret to this little riddle is to read the first word as "not." The message then quickly reads, "Not everyone will get it."*

actually worked with a business coach to help you further your career. In each case, the coach helped to focus and guide you to your goals.

Many professional coaches already know a lot about the Equity Equation and the value of the Hidden Paycheck. They know how to work the equation to make certain that their people are playing at their peak performance. You too can be a coach. As a coach, paying the Hidden Paycheck to your employees becomes a very natural part of what you do every day. If you stop thinking about "managing" people and start thinking about "coaching" them, you will be able to look at your work relationships in a completely different light. And, obviously, as a coach, you'll be pre-disposed to motivating your team to the ultimate goal – to win.

Coaching: The Pre-Requisites

You've got to have three qualities to be a successful coach. They are:

- A "nose for talent" that fits your team
- The ability to focus on people's strengths, not their weaknesses
- A knack for storytelling that both teaches and motivates

A "Nose For Talent" That Fits Your Team

Coaching a winning team is hard work. You are going to have to invest a lot of time and effort into paying your people their long overdue Hidden Paycheck. It only makes sense that you make this investment in the best talent you can find.

The problem today is that so many of us rely on someone else to find the people we hire to be on our teams (human resources, executive search firms, temp agencies, etc.). We tend to neglect the importance of our own role in the hiring process. We look to others to handle the screening and selection process. We depend on them to build the "best" talent pool and then choose for us the best of the best. Unfortunately, many of us have found ourselves left with just what's at the bottom of the barrel.

From the perspective of an athletic coach, this would be like trying to build a championship team made up of just walk-ons. A coach wouldn't try to bring on just any player without first having a thorough understanding of their talent, abilities and whether they were a fit for the team. Nor should you as a leader hire someone who isn't a fit for your own unique corporate culture. All of us have known some extremely talented people who, despite being the best at what they do, failed to bring value to their company/team because they couldn't work well within that particular group dynamic. It is critical that the talent you hire be able to "fit in" with the rest of your team.

Having an instinct for spotting talent doesn't just mean you just screen the people who show up at your office door. If you meet people who could be a good fit, seek them out, create a relationship with them. Maybe they're not looking for a new job right now, or maybe you don't have an opening at the moment. But there's always the future, and it can't hurt to stay in touch. Your needs or theirs might change, and then, who knows, maybe, just maybe, the two of you can work something out.

You, as a coach, need to take an active role as to who is hired to play on your team. You are the person best suited to decide who has the right skills, drive and talent to fit with your team and help you win the game. Don't offer anyone a contract that you have only just met during an interview and who is only one out of three candidates. Take time to make the best choice possible. It will make your working relationships much stronger in the long run – and much more profitable. It's only fair that you (and the person you are hiring) work out the best possible arrangement. After all, it's simply a matter of equity.

The Ability To Focus On People's Strengths, Not Their Weaknesses

Coaches bring out the best in people by focusing on their strengths, not their weaknesses. A coach wouldn't ask their best kicker to also be a defensive lineman, or, a concert pianist to sing rock & roll, or, a dash specialist to become a marathoner.

All of this seems obvious, yet these types of mistakes are being committed over and over again in many different organizations. Why? Companies take for granted what people can already do well and focus on "fixing" what the company considers to be their "weaknesses." The following story makes an important point.

Once upon a time, several animals in a forest decided to open a school. The "students" included a fish, an eagle, a squirrel, and a rabbit. They established a curriculum that included running, swimming, tree climbing, jumping and flying – all of the things that would help them become well-rounded animals.

On the first day of school, the rabbit went to the running class, where he was a star. He happily ran up the hill and down again to easily win the race. The rabbit thought to himself, "I can't believe it! School is great! I get to come here every day and do what I do best!"

The instructor said, "Rabbit, you have a great talent for running. You have great muscles in your rear legs and, with some training, you'll get even better."

The rabbit replied, "I love school! I get to do what I do best and I get to learn how to do it even better."

His second class was swimming. As soon as the rabbit saw the pool and smelled the chlorine, he said,

"I'm not so sure about this class. Rabbits don't like to swim."

The instructor said, "You may not like it now, but years from now, you'll look back and think it was a good thing you learned to swim."

The rabbit's third class was tree climbing. The rabbit tried several times, but he always fell back to the ground. He did just fine in jumping class, but in his last class – the flying class – he had a real problem. He couldn't stay in the air. The teacher then made him take a psychological test and discovered he needed to be in remedial flying. In remedial flying, the rabbit had to practice jumping off a cliff. The teacher told him, "If you work hard enough, you can succeed."

On the second day of school, the swimming instructor announced, "Today, we jump in the water!"

The rabbit responded, "My parents don't swim, my brothers and sisters don't swim. No other rabbits I know swim. Rabbits don't even like to get wet. I want to drop the course."

The instructor replies, "You can't drop it. Drop/add is over. You either jump in or fail the course."

The rabbit jumped in and panicked. He went down once. He went down twice. Bubbles came up. The instructor saw he was drowning and pulled him up. The other animals had never seen anything quite as ridiculous as the wet rabbit. They chirped, they hissed, and they laughed at the rabbit. He was more humiliated than he had ever been in his life. He couldn't wait for class to be over that day.

When he went home, he hoped his parents would understand when he said, "I don't like school! I just want to be free to run and jump and not have to do all of the other things we have to do in school."

But his parents said, "If you are going to get ahead as a rabbit, you have to graduate."

"I don't want to graduate," cried the rabbit.

His parents replied, "You are going to graduate whether you like it or not."

The next day, he hopped slowly to school. He remembered that the principal had said that if any of the students ever had a problem, they could always come and talk to him. So, the rabbit went to the principal's office and told him, "I don't like school."

The principal said, "Really! Tell me why."

When the rabbit was through telling his tale, the principal said, "Rabbit, I hear you. I hear you saying you don't like school because you don't like swimming or flying. I think I have diagnosed the problem. I'll tell you what we'll do. You are doing really well in running and jumping. I don't think you need to work on those anymore. What you need to work on is swimming and flying. So, from now on, instead of taking running and jumping every day, you will take two classes each in both swimming and flying."

The rabbit heard this and got sick to his stomach. As he hopped out of the principal's office, he ran into his old friend, the Wise Old Owl. The Old Owl asked, "Why so glum, rabbit?"

The rabbit told the owl what had happened. The Owl replied, "Rabbit, life doesn't have to be this way. We could have schools and businesses where people are allowed to concentrate on what they do best, not what they do worst."

The rabbit was inspired. He promised himself that once he graduated, he would develop his own school where rabbits ran, fish swam, squirrels climbed trees, and birds flew. As he walked down the hall that day he thought to himself, "Now wouldn't that be a great place to be?"

Over the years, we have met many rabbits – people who had been hired because they had incredible talent at what they do, but who ended up working incredibly hard on everything except what they were best at.

Of course, this doesn't mean that you shouldn't offer challenges to your people. You should try to get them to stretch their current skills, develop new ones, and even try new kinds of tasks. However, you can't afford to have your team so occupied with "fixing" their weaker skills that their strengths go to waste. Just like a muscle that goes flabby if it's not exercised, the talents people have don't get any better, and could even deteriorate, if they're not given regular workouts.

Focusing on and attempting to fix weaknesses only brings a person or an organization to the level of "average." Plus, if people become obsessed with what they can't do, they end up undermining their confidence in those things that they *can* do well. Think about it, Coach. Average might keep you in the game for a little while, but it'll never let you win.

Want proof? Look to your own experience regarding learning grammar and syntax in school. Did the knowledge of knowing how to conjugate verbs or when to use a semi-colon guarantee that you could go out in the world and become a great writer? No. It did mean you could get your thoughts across in a more or less clear manner, which is important. But are you now famous worldwide for your uplifting prose? Probably not. Many people can write an error-free paper, but only a talented few can write a great story. Many truly gifted writers, including Faulkner and Hemingway, were renowned for having truly terrible grammar and syntax. Their publishing houses didn't dwell on making sure the writing of these literary giants was clean of any grammatical gaffes. The publishers let editors fix those problems, leaving the writers free to do what they did best – create great stories.

As a coach, you need to fix your attention on the strengths of your people. Help them become better and better at doing what they do best. If they are rabbits, coach them to be the best rabbits they possibly can be. If they're great writers, encourage them to tell their stories the best way they know how. Remember, you may be able to manage some weaknesses, but you can't eliminate all of them. So, don't even try. Excellence – truly outstanding performance – is achieved only by making strengths even stronger, while managing weaknesses so that they don't get in the way.

A Knack For Storytelling That Teaches And Motivates

Warren Buffett, Berkshire Hathaway, Inc.'s chairman of the board and world-famous investor, told the following story to his shareholders in his company's 1991 annual report:

> *The role that Charlie and I play in the success of our operating units can be illustrated by a story about George Mira, the one-time quarterback for the University of Miami and his coach, Andy Gustafson. Playing Florida and near its goal line, Mira dropped back to pass. He spotted an open receiver but found his right shoulder in the unshakeable grasp of a*

Florida linebacker. The right-handed Mira thereupon switched the ball to his other hand and threw the only left-handed pass of his life – for a touchdown. As the crowd erupted, Gustafson calmly turned to a reporter on the sidelines and declared: "Now that's what I call coaching."

You may not know Warren Buffet personally, but from his story, you now have a pretty clear picture of the culture he inspires within his organization. It's not hard to figure out how Warren feels about decision-making, risk taking, and his own role as a coach within the company.

Storytelling is the single most powerful form of human communication. It is the primary tool people use to pass on values, core beliefs and lessons learned. Storytelling has been used by every society that has ever existed. It is a mechanism by which to communicate valuable truths learned from the past as well as create powerful visions for the future.

What makes storytelling so powerful? Simple. People love a good story. A good story, one that people enjoy again and again, has four qualities. It:

- Captures people's interest
- Holds their attention
- Ignites their imagination
- Is easily remembered, recalled, and retold

Professional coaches of all kinds know that one of the most powerful tools they have to teach, motivate, and inspire their players is storytelling. They reminisce about championships of the past and what it took to win. They keep a losing team in the game by sharing stories at half time about the greatest comebacks.

Coaches know that we all remember "context" far better than we do "content." They know that stories can connect their team and individual players with achievements of the past in such a way that they pave the way to future success. Coaches also know that stories don't have to be positive to be effective. A good story doesn't have to have a happy ending in order to makes a point.

The key to the art of storytelling is the ability to trigger dramatic and memorable pictures in the mind of the listener. You can do this, too. Just like an athletic coach, you as a leader *AND* coach can use stories to impart your values, visions and beliefs to your employees in a way that is natural, fun and as easy to understand.

Coaching and the Five HP Payoffs

Now that you've picked the best people for your team and you've decided to focus on each person's strengths, we are going to use a bit of storytelling to help apply the five Hidden Paycheck Payoffs to your new role as coach. Follow these stories closely. You'll see exactly how they relate to you, as a leader, in just a little bit.

HP Payoff 1: Changing Perspectives

Suppose a coach has a third-year professional player whose performance of late is pretty ragged and who also isn't working cooperatively with the rest of the team. The team's drive for the championship is stumbling as a result. It's time for a face-to-face talk. As the coach listens, he realizes that his player is upset because he's making less money than some of the newer team members. The coach explains that in order to hire the best talent, the team has to pay top money.

"But there's more," the coach says, staring right into the eyeballs of the unhappy player. " You're actually earning 20% more than most of the other third-year players here. In fact, compared to the players who have been here four years or more, your percentage is even higher."

The coach again looks in the player's eyes, which now seem to be softening. He inwardly takes a deep breath and plunges onward. "You know, your situation could be even better. If your individual performance is good, and I see that you're working well with the rest of the team, you can get a lot more from me and the team owners when you renegotiate next year."

The player ponders, nods, then heads back out onto the field. But, now, he's got a much clearer idea of what he can get from the team if he gives good performance and teamwork – and he wants to succeed. The coach can see that the player has a new spirit, a new determination.

The coach even lets himself fantasize a little about winning the championship.

HP Payoff 2: Promoting Positive Expectations

A music coach is prepping one of his best singers for her first solo performance in a major show. This particular extravaganza features a number of celebrated talents. The young singer has a sparkling voice and the kind of talent, which, if properly nurtured, could turn her into a star. But there's a problem. The coach notices that the singer's first rehearsal performance isn't her best, and that she seems faltering and shy around the show's big names, many of whom she idolizes.

Concerned, her coach pulls her aside. With a warm smile, he tells her, "You have a terrific chance here. You're finally in a show that's worthy of your talents. Everything else you've done in your career has been a warm-up. Now cut loose that great voice of yours and blow them all away."

The singer's shoulders straighten, her head tilts upward. After that, even in her rehearsals, her powerful voice makes the rafters rattle. At the end of the performance, she is called back again and again for standing ovations.

HP Payoff 3: Setting Goals

A track star is struggling to make a comeback after a crippling knee injury. He's been training hard, but his progress has been much slower than he hoped. He's doing everything he used to, and he's working just as hard. Still, he can't match his best time in what has been his best race – the 100-meter. He decides to work with a new coach. On the first day of their working together, the runner explains his frustration while standing in the middle of the track.

The coach says, "OK, but before I say anything, run the 100-meter for me a couple of times."

The runner does what he's asked, and the coach calls him over to the side, nodding and looking pleased.

"Got great news for you," the coach tells the runner with a smile. The runner looks back, puzzled. "Here's the thing. Your knee injury is making getting out of the blocks tougher for you. But once you get moving, you come on strong."

The runner flexes his muscles a little, visibly feeling a little hopeful. "Here's an idea. Instead of worrying about the 100-meter race, let's try the 200-meter. The extra distance may let you make up for your slower start and the additional distance will let you use your power to push through the rest of the race."

It works. Not only does the runner leverage his running strengths to quickly top his best time ever in the 200-meter race, he eventually goes on to set record after record in the event.

HP Payoff 4: Providing Feedback on Performance

A soccer coach is watching his players go through drills and calls them over for some quick feedback. To one, he says, "Romano, good work defending the goal. Your focus is sharp and you're showing great consistency." To another player he says, "You're spot on, as well, Carter. The extra work you've been putting in on controlling the ball is really paying off." Then he addresses all the players: "Good warm-up guys. Now, let's get back out there."

As the practice continues, the coach notices that the team's top player and another new player are going head-to-head, each trying to outdo the other. The competition gets fierce, and finally, they start throwing punches at one another. The coach jumps in and yanks the two players to the side.

"Okay, both of you. Enough," he says, disgusted. "Do 20 laps and hit the showers. You can't pull this stuff on my team. Neither of you are starting on Saturday."

The senior player, shocked, protests. "But coach, I'm the best player you've got! You need me out there."

The coach shakes his head. "If you can't work with the rest of the team, how good you are on your own doesn't matter much. Both of you need to shape up. If you don't, you'll stay on the bench."

Saturday arrives and the team plays extremely well. During the second half, the coach puts both of his benched players back in the game and working together, they score the winning goal.

HP Payoff 5: Offering Novel Rewarding Behaviors

A new little league team had been formed, and the coach knew she had a problem. None of her youngsters had ever played before and most of them would be a little younger and smaller than the other kids in the league. Even if they worked very hard, they weren't likely to win many games that first season. In fact, many of the parents predicted they weren't going to win even a single game.

The coach knew she had to do something to make the kids feel they were doing well and keep up morale. So, she went home and created several trophies: the "Super Hit" bat, the "Great Catch" glove, and the "Home Run" ball. At the end of each game, she announced, three of her little players would earn the right to take home one of the trophies, but only for that week. Then the trophies were again up for grabs at the end of the next game. She knew that even when her team took a terrible thumping, the kids would feel their hard work and effort was being valued and appreciated.

To the surprise of most, the coach actually led her undersized team to three straight wins at the end of the season.

OK, so how can these examples apply to you on the business playing field? Imagine if you will, the following:

- What if the third year player who needed to change his perspective in regard to his financial equity was actually a disgruntled employee on your research team?
- What if the singer needing more positive expectations was actually one of your top regional directors who was extremely nervous about giving her first presentation at a national conference?
- What if the track star needing to set new and better goals was actually a salesperson you had rehired who had been out of the industry for a few years and was trying to adapt to new clients and a changed marketplace.
- What if the soccer team needing both positive and developmental feedback was actually your national marketing team with two competing regional sales managers?
- What if the little league team in need of some novel rewarding behaviors was actually a new start-up company trying to gain a foothold in the industry?

For the coaches in our examples, paying the Hidden Paycheck came naturally. It's an expected part of their job. They were there to inspire the best performance possible from their players. All it takes is thinking less like a "manager" and more like a coach.

The Essence Of Give-To-Get Leadership

As you focus on your relationships with your people, here are a few final thoughts:

FIRST, the past decade of increased downsizing and merger activity has brought about the collapse of the old workplace contract...

If you work hard and take care of the company,
the company will take care of you.

With the loss of the workplace contract, people at all levels started feeling they were putting into the company a lot more than they were getting out of it. Not surprisingly, many employees started feeling Under-Rewarded at work. So, they decided to balance the scales by putting less of their head and very little of their heart into their jobs. In short, they did what they had to do, while refusing to give the extra ooommppph (discretionary effort) to their work. Why? Because they didn't want to.

At a time when many organizations only pay lip service to valuing their employees while continuing to chop jobs through downsizing and M&A strategies, you can choose to take a contrarian approach. Instead of leaving your employees disheartened, discouraged and demoralized, you can actually show you value your people by focusing on coaching employees, encouraging them to give the best they've got. Although a lot of people haven't picked up on the message yet, Give-To-Get Leadership will prove to be the most effective and sustainable way to boost stock price in the long term.

SECOND, You, as the immediate manager/leader, should look in the mirror. There you will see the single most important factor in shaping how your people see their job and the organization. You also have the most impact on how well – or poorly – they perform at work. Like setting a thermostat to adjust temperature in a room, you, as a leader, set the "temperature" for your team.

THIRD, it is the *perception* of equity that counts in relationships. And, perceptions are fragile, unpredictable things. How your employee's perceive their Equity Equation is the most critical factor in determining the success or failure of the workplace relationship.

FOURTH, there are four reasons the Equity Equation is difficult to manage: the challenge of building high trust relationships with your employees; the challenge of managing their hidden expectations; the challenge of minimizing stamp collecting; and the challenge of not using the wrong psychological currency with your employees and actually giving them what they actually want from the work relationship.

FIFTH, if you're going to let your employees cash in the Hidden Paycheck, there are five **H**idden **P**aycheck **Payoffs** you can use to rebalance your employees' Equity Equation. These Payoffs offer practical solutions to improving performance by helping alter your employees' perceptions of their workplace relationships and by giving them the payoffs they want from work.

SIXTH, you have to rethink your role as a leader. What separates productive, satisfying work relationships from those in which people grudgingly give just enough to get paid is a very fine edge. In your case, that edge could be the small but clear change in the way you lead – by being less like a manager and more like a coach. Even small changes will have a profound impact on how the people who work for you respond to you.

These ideas may not guarantee full and total perfection in your workplace relationships. But, by giving people more of what they want from their work (paying them the Hidden Paycheck), you will get more of what you want from them – better performance and profit. That's the essence of **Give-To-Get Leadership**.

It's a terrible thing to look over your shoulder when you are trying to lead…

…and find no one there.

– Franklin D. Roosevelt

Chapter 10
Why Me, Why Now?

At this point, you may be looking at these pages and asking yourself...

Do I really want to do this and become a Give-to-Get Leader?

Give-to-Get Leadership isn't easy. To make it work, it will require your commitment, time and practice. You may be in a company where you don't really think your becoming a better leader will make a difference. You yourself may be giving to your organization much more than you are getting and considering all of the other things you have to do everyday, is it really worth your time and effort to pay your employees their Hidden Paycheck when you yourself aren't getting *your* Hidden Paycheck?

You are the only one who can answer these questions. We would only recommend the following: if you are in a job where you honestly feel that you can't make a difference and where you are not motivated to increase both your own effectiveness and the performance of your employees – find something else to do. You will only be contributing more to the problem and will never be part of the solution. Things are probably never going to get better and will most likely get worse. For your own sake, end the relationship and get out.

On the other hand, if you truly feel the desire to make a difference, both in your organization and with your team, it is well worth the effort for you to become a Give-to-Get Leader. Even in the most oppressive work environments, progress and improvement have to start somewhere. Why not with you? At the very least, you'll know you're trying to make a difference for yourself, for your team, and, in time, perhaps for the entire organization. At best, you can be the spark, the person who sets the place on fire, inspiring Give-to-Get Leadership in the very heart of your current corporate culture – or wherever else your career may take you.

Not convinced yet that becoming a Give-To-Get Leader is the path for you. Well, let's take one more look at why the business world today demands a new approach to leadership – one that feeds a different kind of hunger.

A Different Kind of Hunger

It is estimated that over 31 million people in the United States go to sleep hungry every night. It's a real tragedy, especially when you consider that there is no overall food shortage in this country and there isn't any real reason *anyone* should go hungry. But, unfortunately, solving this hunger problem is beyond the scope of this particular book.

What is within our grasp, however, is helping the even millions more out there who are suffering from a different kind of hunger, one just as necessary to human existence as the need for food. These millions of people go to bed every night dreaming about satisfying the most neglected need we all have – the hunger for simple recognition and appreciation from their fellow human beings.

It doesn't matter if you're worth millions or you're struggling to live paycheck-to-paycheck, there is a universal hunger to have our personal worth as individuals confirmed by others – to be appreciated, to be recognized. This is at the very heart of why people are so receptive to receiving their long overdue Hidden Paycheck. People spend so much time and effort on the job, it shouldn't come as any surprise that they are looking to get some recognition and acknowledgment for the work they do each and every day.

As we have said all along, you, as a leader, are the person who can satisfy this hunger in your employees. You are the key to providing people with a sense of personal worth on the job and you can let them know that they are valuable to both you and to your company.

And, guess what? You, as their leader, have an infinite reserve of recognition and acknowledgement currency that you can give out. Don't be stingy with it. Don't ration your praise and appreciation. What are you saving it for? It won't run out. The currency of recognition and appreciation are inexhaustible.

And, don't think you can over-do praise and recognition – that your employees will get sick of hearing how well they are doing and how they are helping to build a great future for the entire team. Think back to the Feedback Gap we told you about earlier. Remember, while managers "almost always" thought that they gave positive feedback for a job well done, their employee reported they only "seldom" were given praise for a job well done. When there is a 200% difference between what you think you, as a leader, are giving to your employees and what they think they are receiving, you aren't in any danger of going overboard on recognition and praise. In other words, people will always want their Hidden Paycheck just as they'll always want their real paycheck.

So, the next time one of your employees does a good job, say so right away and count on the fact that the Hidden Paycheck Currencies you give will mean a lot to the person you are giving it to. Subconsciously, we all know that we only notice what is important to us. Sailors pay close attention to the weather, brokers watch the markets, seniors track health care costs, etc. So, by paying attention and recognizing your employees, you prove to them that they are important to you and that's an equity payoff everyone can appreciate.

And today, this payoff of personal recognition is more important than ever. Technology is encroaching on more and more of the workday (emails, pagers, cell phones, etc.). Direct human interaction (face time) is becoming a scarce commodity and it is one we all increasingly value. ***The age of high tech demands leaders focus even more on high touch relationships.***

As a leader, your willingness to place a priority on your relationships with employees and offer them the recognition and respect that is inherent in the Hidden Paycheck, will be all the more appreciated by those who work for you – and will be all the more powerful when it comes to getting the performance you want from your people.

So, you're it. You are the key to paying your people their Hidden Paycheck.

Times Are Changing

Then there's that other nagging question: "Why should I do this now?"

You might think the leaders at the top of your organization aren't the kind of people who will ever value Give-to-Get Leadership. You may think you're like the person we heard about who tried numerous times to contribute thoughts at staff meetings. Her manager finally pulled her aside and said, "You've got to keep your mouth shut. The people running this company don't want new ideas and they don't want to hear them."

Well, they'd better start listening. Times are changing fast, and your ability to be a Give-to-Get Leader will become a major advantage, either where you are now or where you're going.

Think you're alone? Think you might be the only voice calling out for giving employees a fair shake? Surprise. You've got some company – big and powerful company.

The kings of shareholder value are the institutional investors. You know, the banks, the pension funds, the mutual funds, the places with a lot of money and a lot of clout. They've always been the bean counters, the ones who demand that the companies in which they invest have substantial profits and a hefty stock price. Two highly influential institutions in particular, the Council of Institutional Investors (CII) who manage more than $1 trillion in stocks, and the California Public Employees Retirement System (CalPERS), which manages more than $260 billion worth of investments, have their fingers on the pulse of business life in this country. It's their job. And when *they* talk, other investment people stop and listen.

In the past, neither CII nor CalPERS had ever bothered with issues that many hard-nosed business types considered "the soft stuff," topics like employee satisfaction and loyalty. All that used to matter to these two institutions was the bottom line.

Recently, however, these two financial giants have done a 180-degree turn. CII and CalPERS held a meeting in Washington, D.C. to chew over what they called "good workplace practices." Specifically, they were trying to identify ways to encourage the companies they invested in – and yes, this is true – to value employee satisfaction and loyalty as aids to profitability. In other words, some of the world's most influential investors are starting to look at the ways companies treat their employees as a means of calibrating their future money making potential.

The waves caused by these two giants of finance could swamp those organizations that don't learn to value their employees. If companies don't realize on their own that they need to focus on rebalancing the Equity Equation for their employees, their major investors may force them to do it. Or, they may simply throw the management overboard.

You don't have to wait. Regardless of whether your organization gets the message now or down the line, you can make change now. Consider the possible consequences if you don't.

The Danger in Delay

During the middle ages, scurvy was a deadly scourge claiming the life of many a sailor. Then, in 1601, an English captain, James Lancaster, discovered that eating citrus would prevent scurvy. During the next 150 years, his discovery that sailors who ate lemons and limes avoided the dread disease was ignored. In 1747, a major study by a British naval doctor reached the same conclusion. Despite the mountain of evidence that a sufficient supply of lemons and limes on board ship would keep droves of sailors from dying, the British Navy took another 50 years to make eating lemons and limes at sea mandatory for sailors.

The cost: While the British Navy dithered for half a century, 200,000 of its sailors died of scurvy in that 50 year period. Astonishingly, the British Merchant Marine required an additional 75 years of deliberation before it adopted a similar policy.

You don't have to wait for the top brass in the upper executive suites to deny, dither and ponder before they get around to declaring that employee loyalty actually matters. You can ensure your personal survival right now. Embrace Give-to-Get Leadership and you will have given yourself the best employment security anyone can have in this tempestuous marketplace: The ability to inspire the performance and profit you and your organization want by giving employees what they really want from their jobs.

What employees across the country have made abundantly clear is that they want more balance in their Equity Equation at work. They've gotten the short end of the stick for far too long. Now, they want payback. They want their Hidden Paycheck. And, Give-to-Get Leadership is how you can pay it to them. In return, you'll get the performance you want and need to succeed.

If you're willing to commit yourself to the basic tenets of Give-To-Get Leadership, then you have in your hand the key to unlocking success in any job, any industry, anywhere.

Why not start right now?

For more information about Give-To-Get Leadership including...

- Ordering copies of this book at quantity pricing
- Customizing this book by including adding your own foreword and company information
- Scheduling keynote presentations and motivational seminars based on Give-To-Get Leadership
- Assessing leadership effectiveness in your organization using an Equity-based instrument, and
- Using Give-To-Get Coaching with your leadership team

...contact us at

www.givetogetleadership.com.

Appendix A
Give-To-Get High Payoff Practices

If you have read this book, you know how we all, yourself included, keep a running track of what we are give and what we are getting in our work relationships. We constantly (if only subconsciously) calculate and recalculate our Equity Equation and, more often than not, people believe that the companies they work for aren't holding up their end of the give-to-get bargain.

This book has been focused on managing the Equity Equation within the direct relationship between individual leaders and their employees. As we pointed out in Chapter 6, the immediate manager/leader has the most significant impact on an employee's perception of equity on the job. But that doesn't mean that individual leaders should operate in a vacuum.

There are many other practices that, if implemented at an organizational level, can also help rebalance the Equity Equation for employees in the workplace. These practices can provide an important foundation for individual leaders throughout the organization to maximize their efforts in paying the Hidden Paycheck to their employees. We call these practices, **High Payoff Practices**. High Payoff Practices are designed to create a culture built on the principles of the Equity Equation and Give-To-Get Leadership.

In the remainder of this appendix, we will present a total of ten organizational High Payoff Practices that are all grounded in Equity and are geared toward providing employees with more of the Outcomes they seek in their relationship with their organizations. These Give-To-Get High Payoff Practices are how organizations as a whole can pay their employees their Hidden Paycheck.

High Payoff Practice 1
Vision & Alignment

Create vision and alignment that inspires, motivates and celebrates your people.

Many business leaders "talk" endlessly about vision, and your organization probably has its own version of a vision or a mission statement. But does it address and engage your employees? Usually, if employees are mentioned at all, the subject is addressed in the most glancing manner. This fact is astonishing considering that if the company ever hopes to achieve the goals it has for the future, it'll be their employees who will get them there. Not customers. Not shareholders. Employees. All of them.

Look at it in terms of the Equity Equation. If people are going to jump out of bed ready to hit the ground running each morning – to give their best – they need to know where it is that they're running to. They need a road map. Without it, people feel they are working very hard and getting nowhere. In addition, if they feel that vision doesn't include them, if it doesn't CELEBRATE their contribution to the organization and its future success, then why would they bother working toward it? Remember, we all like to feel that we are part of a winning team. Make sure that your vision acknowledges that all of the players in your company will help make that win possible.

A strong vision is the first step in getting people motivated to perform their best. The second step is making sure that the work being done day-to-day, all of the policies, procedures, and processes in your company, are aligned with that vision. For employees, there is nothing worse than coming into work and knowing that the meeting they have to go to that day or the reports that they have to fill out at the end of each quarter, do nothing to actually achieve any real business goals.

Even worse is when company policies become so time consuming and cumbersome that they actually stop employees from doing what they really need to do in order to achieve organizational goals.

A vision is a powerful motivator for any organization or team – as long as all employees are part of it and what they're doing is actually in line with achieving it.

High Payoff Practice 2
Learning and Innovation Culture

Cultivate an environment that values, recognizes and rewards learning more, and more quickly, than the competition and leveraging new and better practices throughout the organization.

Where will organizations find their sustainable competitive advantage in the future? Technology? Merger? Downsizing? Highly unlikely. Today, the true value of an organization comes from creating new knowledge that can be translated into more efficient ways of doing business. Not too surprisingly, the best resource any company has for new ideas is its own workforce. If companies can nurture a workforce where employees can not only learn and develop new ideas, but are also encouraged to do so, these companies will be able to capitalize on untold opportunities in the future.

How does this concept fit into the Equity Equation? Wonderfully. When learning, creativity and innovation, along with the sharing of knowledge, is valued, recognized and rewarded by the organization, all kinds of ideas will spring up – because employees know that the organization appreciates and encourages new thinking. Give people encouragement and reward for doing something you want them to do and they'll keep on doing it, and more of it. One way of showing employees that this new thinking is valued is to give them the time and opportunity to develop themselves and share what they have learned.

Now, many companies say that's what they do. These are the same companies who believe that a suggestion box is sufficient to encourage input from employees. It isn't. In fact, a corporate culture where learning is genuinely welcomed hardly ever exists. The reality is that employees find that they're so caught up in getting the day-to-day tasks done that there's no time left over to learn anything new.

Or, if employees do have ideas, the organizational culture frequently finds ways to sabotage their speaking out. If a company wants experimentation, new ideas and practices, then it has to convince its people that if they contribute new ideas or practices that actually are put into effect, the organization will recognize and reward the people who created them.

High Payoff Practice 3
Transparent Score Keeping

Have widespread sharing of financial and performance information in formats that let employees know the score.

Why do most of us love to watch and play various sports and games? We like to win. How do we know we are winning? We keep score.

Imagine you're playing a game where you had no way of knowing if you are winning or losing the game – playing tennis without a net, playing football without goal posts or yard line markers, etc. If you never knew whether you were winning or losing, how motivated would you be to take risks, go after a big play or devise a winning strategy? If you never knew the score, how long would you keep playing before you got bored, frustrated and walked away? Not long.

While most of us realize the importance of keeping score when it comes to sports and games, it's amazing how many corporations try and win without ever telling their players the score. Many employees show up to work every day without knowing whether their "team" is winning or losing. Developing a clear and easily understood score keeping system is the key to keeping peoples' "heads in the game." Unless they are so far behind that they are out of the game, people tend to play harder when they know the score and what they have to do to win.

So, what exactly is "transparent score keeping?" It's measuring the critical behaviors which can help or hurt the bottom-line in ways that are:

- Simple
- Clear
- And easy for all to see

Basically, a transparent score keeping system is like a scoreboard at a football game – an easy way to see the most essential information about the game. In a flash, you'll know who's playing, the current score, the time remaining to play and the current conditions of the game. You only need take a quick look at the board to know who is winning the game and who isn't.

Everyone on your team needs to be motivated to win the game. Again, go back to the Equity Equation. If employees give their hard work, their skills, and their commitment, they deserve to get feedback on their performance in a timely and easily understood format. That's what transparent score keeping is all about.

High Payoff Practice 4
Financial Incentives

Offer competitive pay with financial incentives that are driven deep into the organization – everyone gets to share. Reward not only good execution, but innovation, as well.

Just because we're targeting the Hidden Paycheck doesn't mean that the one that pays the mortgage, buys the car and puts the kids through college can be ignored. Pay is still the primary reason most of us get out of bed in the morning to face the hours of work ahead of us. No one would want to deny the power money has to prompt and reward terrific performance. Indeed, many corporations already offer financial incentives, but usually only to the top people in the organization – primarily, CEOs and other top-level executives reap the rewards that come from strong corporate performance.

As we mentioned earlier, in 1999, the average CEO of a major corporation earned more then 475 times that of the average factory worker. When people perceive an imbalance in equity -- and pay certainly is the kind of imbalance that shows up very quickly on their radar screens – it drastically reduces their willingness to perform. It saps their willingness to do their jobs fully and well. If people aren't motivated to excel at their jobs, performance doesn't skyrocket, it sputters, and the bottom line suffers accordingly. But, for those companies – few though they may be – who have realized the power of distributing financial incentives across the organization, have watched their bottom lines flourish.

The concepts of competitive pay and financial incentives have to be driven so deeply into the organization that even the people at the lowest levels have a chance to reap the benefits. All employees – from the mailroom to the executive suite – have to feel that if their team or their company does well, then they themselves will get a slice of the pie. That's what financial equity means to you, doesn't it? If that's what it means to you, then why would the people who report to you, or the people who report to them, feel any differently?

Oh, there's a little postscript here. Remember High Payoff Practice 2 – the one about cultivating an environment that values, recognizes and rewards learning and innovation? Well, don't just make those words sound pretty. Back them up with hard cash. People should get good bucks for creativity and innovation as well as for the number of transmissions produced by an assembly line or the number of computers shipped.

High Payoff Practice 5
Selective & Secure Employment

Promote long-term employee relationships through selective, lean and focused hiring.

First, you must "hire the best and fire the worst." You may have heard this adage many times before but we can't emphasize its value enough. In reality, most companies do much better at "hiring the best" than they do at "firing the worst."

You may be surprised to learn that this value is one that's also based on equity. If your very best people see that your organization is willing to tolerate substandard work from other people around them, and these people get to stay on the job, that fact sends a message, and it is this: "Lousy work tolerated here."

Not the most inspiring message, is it? All it does is get your very best people to take the edge off performances that used to be razor-sharp. If the company doesn't care enough about the quality of the work to toss out the people who don't do the job, then why should the people who can do the job well make the effort?

Second, providing employment security is absolutely vital for motivating people to perform their very best. Employees who are distracted by worries over what will happen to them if they lose their job simply can't focus on doing their best work. Lean and selective hiring requires that organizations, yours included, fill empty slots with the utmost care and consideration. It's essential to comb through roles and responsibilities inside the organization constantly, then decide which jobs are essential and who the best people are to fill them.

We advise teams and companies to retool themselves often. By trying to create new synergies between existing roles and responsibilities, a company can beef up its effectiveness while at the same time giving employees a chance to stretch their talents and create an even larger number of skills and wider experience in the process.

For example, if a position opens up, don't automatically fill it. First, ask the people in the same area whether the job is really needed or if there's a more effective way to get the job done. If the work can be consolidated among existing employees or several open positions combined into just a few new ones, the people taking on the work must be compensated for the extra work. If employees are willing to help save the company money by doing more, then they should be rewarded. That's one way financial equity is distributed among your people, along with the new responsibilities. Getting more pay for helping have fewer jobs is one way to make sure that selective, lean hiring actually works.

High Payoff Practice 6
Decentralized Decision Making

Sponsor self-managed teams with informal leadership empowered to make decisions close to the point of transaction, be it with customers, vendors or partners.

Today, change is a given. It's rampant in organizations and the marketplace. As a result, the ability to make decisions rapidly becomes essential. Wasting time frequently means wasting opportunity. Companies don't have the luxury of passing ideas up and down the corporate ladder before someone – anyone – finally makes a decision.

Instead of allowing your people to fritter away their time dithering over who will make the decision and what the decision will be, just give the person in your company closest to the point of transaction – whether it's with a customer, partner or vendor – the authority to take charge and make decisions. The people closest to the situation obviously know the most about what's going on and are best suited to make the right choices. So let them do it.

But, be warned. If you do decentralize decision-making, you must do it on a basis of trust. Don't make the same mistake many companies make. While they say they believe the people down the ladder making the decisions are, generally, making the right choices, they actually inwardly cringe at the thought of decentralizing decision-making, fearing it will lead to bad decisions. Sure there's some risk of this, but it's largely offset by the increased response time to both change and opportunity. Incidentally, just where is it carved in stone that because someone at the top makes a decision that success is necessarily guaranteed?

Trust is essential to carry off decentralization. Though many companies now mumble soothing words about how their employees are empowered, employees who exercise that power on a day-to-day basis often find themselves being overruled by their superiors in the organization. These superiors constantly question and/or revoke the decisions their subordinates make and often, when things go bad, employees find themselves being punished for doing what they thought was their job.

The concept really is simple. When employees are hired to do a job, they want to know that they're trusted to do it well. What they don't want is the uneasy feeling that just around the corner, a manager is waiting to jump on them if they actually do make decisions or something goes wrong with the decisions they've made.

Employees should be held accountable for their decisions, sure. But it's only fair that the organization respect the decisions they make or provide the training/knowledge required to make the right decisions.

Again, it's a question of equity. If employees feel their intelligence and ability to make sound decisions really isn't respected or supported by their organization, they'll go back to doing just enough to get by and avoid making any decisions at all. That way they get their paychecks and take no risk. It's a safe, secure approach to keeping a job, but it also means a lot of missed opportunity for the company.

High Payoff Practice 7
Reduce Status Distinctions

Level off excessive "perks" which create barriers between leaders and the people they are trying to lead.

This practice may seem simplistic but it plays a very important role in rebalancing the equity equation for employees. We are not saying that employees want their CEO to work out of the cubical next to theirs. Most employees understand that their bosses will make more money or get more stock options, or even some other perks. But, these extras need to be seen as competitively justified or tied to the business.

When the top brass proudly hang a newly purchased piece of art in the lobby purchased with corporate funds or throw a swanky party celebrating a recent merger on a yacht only days after announcing layoffs, this destroys the sense of equity in the organization. It is surprising how easily executives delude themselves into thinking they are entitled to privileges that are neither necessary to their jobs nor appropriate perks of their station. It goes way beyond obscene salaries and huge options; it's about a form of corporate elitism that chokes off employees' desire to use their discretionary effort.

Even little perks like reserved parking, corner offices, or lofty titles can seem on the surface to be acceptable corporate rewards, but these status distinctions can have a nasty consequence – they cut leaders off from the very people they are trying to lead, inhibiting open communication and interaction.

The perks that come from status distinctions may seem like "just desserts" to the people who receive them, but what they often end up doing is creating envy and resentment in those who are lower down on the corporate ladder. There is food for thought in the old adage,

You will never impress those who have more and will only stir envy in those who have less.

Inappropriate perks often lead people away from focusing on the job at hand. Internal competition sparked by the distribution of "perks" often causes people to focus on aspects of equity that are unproductive and unprofitable. Bitter thoughts like, "If she has that title, so should I!" or "I've been here longer but he got the office with a window." Reducing status distinctions and distributing "perks" equitably creates a more level playing field between leaders and their employees so that everyone can focus on the real work to be done.

High Payoff Practice 8
High Value Training & Education Programs

Provide training and education programs aligned with business goals that maximize overall performance, enhance employee marketability, and promote long-term employee relationships.

If a company closely aligns training and education programs with business goals, they can make certain their employees are kept up to speed on the skills and knowledge necessary for the company to be successful and prosperous. That's one benefit.

But, high value training and educations programs can also be an equitable compromise companies can offer their employees. While it is now nearly impossible for companies to promise their people "employment for life," they can promise employees they will keep them employable – providing appropriate training and education that will allow employees to broaden and improve their own skills. This training and education enhances their performance in their current job, but also keeps them competitive in the marketplace. So, if employee and company do part paths, the company has at least equipped that person to land another good job.

There's also a bonus for those companies genuinely trying to build long-term relationships with their employees. Data from the 1999 Emerging Workforce Study shows that 41% of employees who say their company offers poor training plan to look for another job within 12 months. But just 12% of those who rated training opportunities as excellent within their organizations expected to jump ship. As many companies know, high turnover isn't cheap. That same survey pegged the cost of losing the typical worker at $50,000.

When times are good, most companies do a reasonable job of providing quality training and education programs to their employees. However, when the economy gets iffy, training and education programs are among the first casualties on the cost-cutting chopping block.

Before you cut training and education, consider if the money you save will outweigh the equity cost to your employees. Is it better to prove to your employees that you value them enough to continue growing their knowledge and skill levels or do you want to risk alienating them and losing their top performance?

High Payoff Practice 9
Stretch Assignments

Employee development through carefully selected on-the-job "stretch & growth" assignments supported by mentoring and coaching.

Over the years, we have asked hundreds of successful leaders in all types of companies one very basic question: "As you look back, what has contributed most to your growth and development as a leader?" Far and away the most frequent answer is "...when I was given a stretch assignment."

Stretch assignments are challenging jobs that are given to employees so that they may "stretch" their skills and abilities to levels not achieved before. Stretch assignments present new and difficult challenges to executives. They're tough. But, if employees survive and complete these assignments successfully, they are rewarded with greater confidence in their leadership ability as well as having learned new skills. In study after study, people say that they learn most effectively while they are on-the-job. If challenging tasks push the limits of the employee's knowledge and abilities, then the company as well as the employee benefit enormously.

Many companies already utilize stretch assignments quite effectively. A recent study by McKinsey & Company entitled *Winning the War for Talent*, asked managers how effective their particular company was at utilizing stretch assignments as a development tool. Most executives gave their companies a very high rating.

However, not all stretch assignments end well, especially if handled badly. They are often stress-filled and can lead a once high potential employee to ruin. Companies cannot simply throw their people into tough positions and then simply expect them to do well. They need to offer support to their employees and help them either learn or develop the skills necessary to do the job right. What's the key? Most leaders say that the difference between success and failure during a stretch assignment is the availability of coaching and feedback from their immediate manager.

High Payoff Practice 10
Coaching & Feedback

Having the immediate manager provide coaching and feedback on issues of performance and development makes all the difference.

This practice is the most important of all – that's why it's been the focus of this book. It's the immediate manager who is the direct connection between employees and the rest of the organization. The McKinsey study we referred to earlier also found that while managers frequently say that coaching and feedback are the most important support a company can offer to their development, companies consistently do a poor job of providing it. People who go about their daily routine seldom are told what they're doing right, or what they're doing wrong, and how, if possible, to do it better.

Why coaching? Think about it. Would you rather be coached or managed? A manager tells you what tasks what you need to do and then makes sure you get it done. If you're lucky, they might sit down with you once a year and give you a very general review of your performance. A coach on the other hand, would tell you what needs to be done, help you build the skills you need to do it, let you know immediately if you are doing it right (or wrong), and be there to encourage you the entire way.

Coaching and feedback is the critical link between managers and direct reports. This relationship, in turn, is the conduit for all the other Give-to-Get High Payoff Practices.

The Final Word

Please note, an organization that tries to pay its people the Hidden Paycheck fully and often in order for employees to feel they're giving as good as they're getting, will reap the benefits. However, if a company has the mechanics in place to deliver High-Payoff Practices, but its leaders don't use them or act to sabotage them, then those practices won't pay off much at all.

It's the same at an individual level. If you're trying to deliver the Hidden Paycheck so your people can get what they want from their work, but your organization doesn't help you do it, then of course you'll find delivering that Hidden Paycheck more difficult.

We know that there are many managers/leaders who aren't in a good position to affect their organization's policy. If that's your situation, take heart. You can still give employees a fair shake from day to day.

How?

Please look closely at Part II of this book again. There you'll find a huge stash of ideas and techniques showing what you, as an individual manager/leader can do to distribute the Hidden Paycheck to your people. No matter what the rest of the organization is doing, you can get the high performance and the steady profit you need to make – your team, your company and you – productive, satisfied and successful.

Appendix A

End Notes

Chapter 1

Most authors on leadership focus on traits or characteristics that effective leaders should possess. Our discussion of traditional versus contrarian models of leadership development is derived in part from David V. Day's article "Leadership Development: A Review In Context" which appeared in *Leadership Quarterly*, 11, 4, 581-613 (2001).

Chapter 2

Fortune magazine has published a list of the largest companies in the United States and in the world since 1972. This list has recently become available on the Internet (http://www.fortune.com) and is searchable by industry, country, SIC code and numerous other variables.

The principles of reengineering were derived from Michael Hammer and James Champy's *Reengineering the Corporation: A Manifesto for Business Revolution*, HarperBusiness (1993).

Annual extended mass layoff data provided by the U.S. Department of Labor Bureau of Labor Statistics via their website at http://stats.bls.gov. Additional information provided by public downsizing/job cut announcements made by the executive search firm Challenger, Grey and Christmas and as reported in publications like *The New York Times* and *Reuters*.

Percentages of companies who engaged in downsizing as a result of business downturns were taken from the American Management Association's *Corporate Job Creation, Job Elimination, and Downsizing* (1997).

IBM for many years had a "no layoff" policy. There was a prevailing mindset of "family" at this and other corporations. Thomas Watson, Sr., founder of IBM, was quoted by James Traub in "Loyalty: A Spasm of Layoffs and Downsizing in the 1980's Obliterated What Was Left of Corporate Loyalty" in *Business Month* (October 1990). Other IBM information derived from Richard Sennet's *The Corrosion of Character*, W.W. Norton & Company (1998).

The juxtaposed articles from March 1994 in regard to IBM were taken from Alan Downs' *Corporate Executions* published by AMACOM (1995).

There are numerous articles voicing the concerns over what happens to people after they have been downsized. One good example is "Life After The Heave-Ho" by Janice Revell, *Fortune* (November 27, 2000).

Information regarding Al Dunlap was taken from numerous sources. They included: "Dunlap Has History of Success" by Mary Kane, *The Plain Dealer* (December 31, 1995); "Dunlap's Math: 1 + 1 = 3" by Jim Mitchell, *Dallas Morning News* (July 19, 1995); "Hatchet Man or Savior?" by Barbara Sullivan, *Chicago Tribune* (January 7, 1997); and "Dunlap's Shadow Still Felt At Sunbeam" by Michael Connor, *Reuters* (February 26, 2001).

U.S. and global merger and acquisition data was gathered from articles on CNNfn.com reporting on press releases made by Thompson Financial Corporation.

Data on failed merger and acquisition deals including AT&T/NCR and American Home Produces/Monsanto from Kevin Walker's "Meshing Cultures In A Consolidation," *Training & Development* (May 1998).

In 1995, Mercer Management Consulting and *Business Week* carried out a joint study of post-merger performance for 150 companies that had merged between 1990 and 1995. They found that fully half of the mergers were failures in terms of returns to shareholders relative to industry peers over a three-year period. The reasons for failure were generally found to be conflicting corporate cultures and a slow pace of integration. For more information, see Martin Smye's article "Managing The Human Risks of Bank Mergers," *The Journal of Lending & Credit Risk Management* (July, 1998).

"Corporate America Rebounds," *Business Week* (July 7, 1997) reported how organizations in the U.S. had made a comeback in the global marketplace.

The World Economic Forum has issued a series of Global Competitiveness Reports beginning in 1979, which ranks countries according to high productivity. For more information, see their website at www.weforum.org/publications.

A recent example of the impact of downsizing on employee attitude can be found a *New York Times* article entitled "In a Downsizing, Loyalty Is A Two-Way Street" (April 15, 2001). In this article, one employee stated, "We don't have control over how an organization handles a layoff... but we do have control over how we choose as individuals to respond to it."

Reports of continuing job cuts was reported in the *New York Times* on Sunday, August 5, 2001 in an article entitled "Pink Slip? Now, It's All In A Day's Work" by Louis Uchitelle. Most troubling in this article was a statement by Ronald Blackwell, director of corporate affairs at the AFL-CIO. In terms of layoffs, he said, "... they [employees] see no reason to expect anything different from employers."

John Kelly, KPMG's UK head of Merger and Acquisition Integration, was quoted in *Transaction Services* (April 18, 2001) as saying, "The new wave of corporate activity looks set to be demergers/disposals, with the number of companies considering separation increasing considerably."

Chapter 3

For more information on marriage and divorce rates in the United States, consult the U.S. Census Bureau Statistical Abstract of the United States 2000. An online version of the abstract can be found at www.census.gov.

For more information on the number of people quitting their jobs, consult the Bureau of Labor Statistics via their website at http://stats.bls.gov.

Chapter 4

For further insights on Aristotle's view of the notion of exchange, equity and reciprocity, see his *Nicomachean Ethics* published by Harvard University Press (1926 translation).

In 1989, Richard C. Huseman and John D. Hatfield wrote their book *Managing The Equity Factor… or, "After All I Have Done For You…"* published by Houghton Mifflin, they spoke of "Equity Axioms." After several more years of research and study, we have seen the enormous power and influence of Equity in workplace performance. The three Equity principles are far more than just axioms; therefore, we now refer to them as the three "laws" of Equity.

The data in regard to whether employees felt over-rewarded, equitably rewarded, or under-rewarded came from responses to a survey we have devised entitled The Job Relations Inventory (JRI). These responses came from several thousand employees in some the largest corporations in the world. To find out more about the JRI and its ability to measure both employee perceptions of equity and leadership strategies to increase employee outcomes, please contact the authors at either www.thecoachingedge.com or www.thehayesgroupintl.com.

The problem of identifying "comparison others" is summarized well in Richard T. Mowday's *Equity Theory Predictions of Behavior in Organizations.*

The study of the professors and their unsolicited Holiday cards can be found in Phillip R. Kunx and Micahel Woolrott's "Season's Greetings From My Status To Yours," *Social Science Research* (1976).

The study of baseball players and equity is reported in Robert G. Lord and Jeffrey A. Hohenfeld, "Longitudinal Field Assessment of Equity Effects on the Performance of Major League Baseball Players," *Social Science Research* (1979).

Data in regard to robbery and theft in the fast food industry was taken from Eric Schlosser's *Fast Food Nation: The Dark Side of the American Meal*, Houghton-Mifflin (2001).

Chapter 5

Aldous Huxley's notion of how powerful our perceptual skills are is taken from his book, *The Doors of Perception, and Heaven and Hell*, Harper and Row (1956).

Our data on physical limitations to perception were taken from several sources including David E. Davis, *Integral Animal Behavior*, Macmillan Company (1966); Matthew Alpern, Merle Lawrence, and David Wolsk, *Sensory Perception*, Brooks/Cole Publishing Company (1967); and Willard R. Zemlin, *Speech and Hearing Science*, Englewood Cliffs, Prentice-Hall (1968).

The discussion of turkeys and skunks was adapted from M. W. Fox's *Concepts in Ethology: Animal and Human Behavior*, University of Minnesota Press (1974).

Data on skin cancer came from the American Cancer Society (http://www.cancer.org/statistics). Data on the number of auto accidents came from the Department of Transportation National Highway Traffic Safety Commission (http://www.nhtsa.dot.gov). Data on smoking came from Boston University's Community Outreach Health Information System (http://www.bu.edu/cohis). Data on the number of shark attacks came from the International Shark Attack File (http://www.flmnh.ufl.edu/fish/Sharks/isaf/isaf.htm)

Chapter 6

The data on employees' preferred source of information for the United States, the United Kingdom and Canada was originally found in Julie Foehrenback and Karen Rosenburg's "How Are We Doing?" *Journal of Communication Management*, vol. 12, no. 1 (1983). The original source for GM employees' preferred source of information originally taken from "Local Managers + Information = Key Internal Communicators," *Employee Relations and Human Resources Bulletin*, Report no. 1672, sec. 1, September 21, 1988. Both original findings were reprinted in *Communicating Change*, Larkin & Larkin (1994). Percentages do not add up to 100% as respondents were asked to choose more than one source.

For more detailed findings from the Gallup Study, consult Marcus Buckingham and Curt Coffman's *First, Break All The Rules: What The World's Greatest Managers Do Differently*, Simon & Schuster (1999).

According to *Business Week's* annual survey, the average CEO of a major corporation made $12.4 million in 1999, up 17% from the pervious year. That's 475 times more than an average blue-collar worker and six times the average CEO paycheck in 1990. For more information on the difference between worker and executive compensation information or CEO pay in respect to corporate stock performance, see *Executive Pay Watch* (http://www.aflcio.org/paywatch).

Data in regard to severance packages offered to ousted CEOs from Janice Revell's "Life After The Heave-Ho," *Fortune* (November 27, 2000).

Daniel Yankelovich and John Immerwahr are given credit for first using the term "discretionary effort."

For more information on the ABC Behavior Model, see Aubrey Daniels' *Bringing Out The Best In People* McGraw-Hill (1994) and Leslie Wilk Braksick's *Unlock Behavior, Unleash Profits*, McGraw-Hill (2000).

Chapter 7

The Center for Creative Leadership study was reported in "What Makes for Executive Success," *Psychology Today* (February 1983).

The Boston University study of trust was reported in *USA Today* (May 16, 1987).

The competence/caring model of trust we present is based in part on the work of Peter R. Scholtes as reported in the book, *The Leader's Handbook*, McGraw-Hill (1998).

The term "idiosyncratic credit" was taken from E. P. Hollander, "Conformity, Status and Idiosyncrasy Credit," *Psychology Review* (1958).

Chapter 8

The poem about the blind men trying to figure out the elephant is entitled "The Blind Men and the Elephant" and was written by John G. Saxe.

There are several versions of the Roger Bannister story. The one we site here is from an article entitled "The Extra Plus in Leadership: Attitude" from *Developing the Leader Within You* by John Maxwell. A copy of the article can be found in *The Life@Work Book* from the editors of the *Life@Work Journal* and published by Word Publishing (2000).

At the time of this writing, the world record holder for the one-mile run is Hicham El-Guerroui of Morocco. He established a time of 3:43.13 in Rome on July 7, 1999. El-Guerrouj exploded onto the world scene as a world-class runner in 1994, and since then, has become the man to beat in the 1500m and the mile. He holds both the indoor and outdoor 1500m and one-mile world records.

Using a worm to cure toothaches is an old story. We found it in a book that contains a classic study of the Pygmalion Effect in schools. The book is by Robert Rosenthal and Lenore Jacobson entitled *Pygmalion in the Classroom*, Holt, Rinehart and Winston (1968).

Eliza Doolittle's words are take from G.B. Shaw's *Pygmalion*, Max Reinhardt, Constable (1958).

A review of studies of the Pygmalion Effect can be found in Dov Eden's "Self-Fulfilling Prophecy as a Management Tool," *Academy of Management Review* (1984).

An excellent review and application of goal setting theory is in Edwin Locke's *Goal-Setting: A Motivational Technique That Works!* Prentice-Hall (1984).

For further discussion of Douglas McGregor's Hot Stove Rules, see Leon D. Boncarosky's "Guidelines to Corrective Discipline," *Personnel Journal* (October 1979).

Statistics on hunger in America were taken from George M. Anderson's "Hungry in America, " *America* (April 22, 2000).

Chapter 9

Those in the area of special education have used the story of the rabbit for years. The version of the rabbit story we have used here as well as the example of the great writers with poor spelling and syntax skills was adapted from Donald O. Clifton and Paula Nelson's *Soar With Your Strengths*, Delacorte Press (1992).

The story about quarterback George Mira and his Univerisity of Miami coach Andy Gustafson was adapted from a letter by Warren Buffet to his shareholders on page 5 of the 1991 Berkshire Hathaway Annual Report.

How goal setting and feedback affect motivational and performance levels on soldiers was taken from the book *Encouraging the Heart* by James M. Kouzes and Barry Z. Possner, Jossey-Bass (1999). The original source for this information is from A. Bandura and D. Cervone's "Self-Evaluation and Self-Efficacy Mechanisms Governing the Motivational Effects of Goal Systems," in the *Journal of Personality and Social Psychology*, 1983, 43, 99. 1017-1028.

Chapter 10

Deborah Leff, president of America's Second Harvest, the nation's leading domestic hunger-relief organization said that, "...there are more than 31 million American's who are hungry or at risk of being hungry." Her statement appeared in a PR Newswire article entitled

"Starved for the Facts About Hunger in America" on September 26, 2000.

Information regarding CII and CalPERS and their focus on the importance of employees to a company's total value is taken in part from Marcus Buckingham and Curt Coffman's *First, Break All the Rules: What the World's Greatest Managers Do Differently*, Simon & Schuster (1999).

ABOUT THE AUTHORS

Richard C. Huseman, Ph.D.
rhuseman@sprintmail.com

Dick Huseman serves as an executive coach, keynote speaker, and consultant. He has had a variety of experiences in business school settings, serving as professor, department head, and dean. Working with companies like AT&T, Coca Cola, ExxonMobil, and IBM, his focus has been in the areas of knowledge management, change management, and most importantly, relationship management. Dick has co-authored nine books, including his most recent work, *Leading with Knowledge* (1999), as well as the precursor to this book, *Managing The Equity Factor* (1989), which has been translated into Russian, German, Chinese, Portuguese, and Greek. **Give-To-Get Leadership** is the culmination of 20 years of research and observation as to the true explanation of organizational performance and productivity – equitable relationships.

Merwyn A. Hayes, Ph.D.
merwyn@thehayesgroupintnl.com

Merwyn Hayes has worked as a consultant and executive coach on team and "people" issues for more than 30 years, serving more than 400 clients around the globe. He is known for his practical applications of the concept of **Give-To-Get Leadership** and organizational performance. As one client put it, "Merwyn has the ability to successfully get the tough issues on the table and, although there is conflict, everyone leaves the meeting feeling good about themselves and the results of what has been achieved." His 1994 book, *The Belief System: The Secret to Motivation and Improved Performance*, co-authored with Thad Green, has helped many managers better understand how to successfully motivate others.

The authors have been friends and business colleagues since they met in graduate school.

Printed in the United States
1647